W9-AOE-279

Democracy

Other Books of Related Interest:

At Issue Series

Does the U.S. Two-Party System Still Work?

How Does Religion Influence Politics?

Should the Federal Government Bail Out Private Industry?

Should the U.S. Close Its Borders?

Voter Fraud

What Rights Should Illegal Immigrants Have?

Current Controversies Series

Capitalism

Federal Elections

Introducing Issues with Opposing Viewpoints Series

Civil Liberties

Human Rights

Opposing Viewpoints Series

Political Campaigns

Presidential Powers

Democracy

Tom Lansford, Book Editor

GREENHAVEN PRESS
A part of Gale, Cengage Learning

Detroit • New York • San Francisco • New Haven, Conn • Waterville, Maine • London

Christine Nasso, *Publisher*
Elizabeth Des Chenes, *Managing Editor*

For more information, contact:
Greenhaven Press
27500 Drake Rd.
Farmington Hills, MI 48331-3535
Or you can visit our Internet site at gale.cengage.com

LIBRARY OF CONGRESS CATALOGING-IN-PUBLICATION DATA

Democracy / Tom Lansford, book editor.
p. cm. -- (Global viewpoints)
Includes bibliographical references and index.
ISBN 978-0-7377-4715-7 (hardcover) -- ISBN 978-0-7377-4716-4 (pbk.)
1. Democracy. 2. Democratization. I. Lansford, Tom.
JC423.D381255 2011
321.8--dc22

2010032975

Printed in the United States of America
1 2 3 4 5 6 7 15 14 13 12 11

Contents

Chapter 2: Democracy and Equality

Chapter 3: Democracy and Economics

Chapter 4: Democracy and International Relations

Foreword

> *"The problems of all of humanity can only be solved by all of humanity."*
> *—Swiss author Friedrich Dürrenmatt*

Global interdependence has become an undeniable reality. Mass media and technology have increased worldwide access to information and created a society of global citizens. Understanding and navigating this global community is a challenge, requiring a high degree of information literacy and a new level of learning sophistication.

Building on the success of its flagship series, *Opposing Viewpoints*, Greenhaven Press has created the *Global Viewpoints* series to examine a broad range of current, often controversial topics of worldwide importance from a variety of international perspectives. Providing students and other readers with the information they need to explore global connections and think critically about worldwide implications, each *Global Viewpoints* volume offers a panoramic view of a topic of widespread significance.

Drugs, famine, immigration—a broad, international treatment is essential to do justice to social, environmental, health, and political issues such as these. Junior high, high school, and early college students, as well as general readers, can all use *Global Viewpoints* anthologies to discern the complexities relating to each issue. Readers will be able to examine unique national perspectives while, at the same time, appreciating the interconnectedness that global priorities bring to all nations and cultures.

Material in each volume is selected from a diverse range of sources, including journals, magazines, newspapers, nonfiction books, speeches, government documents, pamphlets, organization newsletters, and position papers. *Global Viewpoints* is truly global, with material drawn primarily from international sources available in English and secondarily from U.S. sources with extensive international coverage.

Features of each volume in the *Global Viewpoints* series include:

- An **annotated table of contents** that provides a brief summary of each essay in the volume, including the name of the country or area covered in the essay.
- An **introduction** specific to the volume topic.
- A **world map** to help readers locate the countries or areas covered in the essays.
- For each viewpoint, an **introduction** that contains notes about the author and source of the viewpoint explains why material from the specific country is being presented, summarizes the main points of the viewpoint, and offers three **guided reading questions** to aid in understanding and comprehension.
- **For further discussion** questions that promote critical thinking by asking the reader to compare and contrast aspects of the viewpoints or draw conclusions about perspectives and arguments.
- A worldwide list of **organizations to contact** for readers seeking additional information.
- A **periodical bibliography** for each chapter and a **bibliography of books** on the volume topic to aid in further research.
- A comprehensive **subject index** to offer access to people, places, events, and subjects cited in the text, with the countries covered in the viewpoints highlighted.

Global Viewpoints is designed for a broad spectrum of readers who want to learn more about current events, history, political science, government, international relations, economics, environmental science, world cultures, and sociology—students doing research for class assignments or debates, teachers and faculty seeking to supplement course materials, and others wanting to understand current issues better. By presenting how people in various countries perceive the root causes, current consequences, and proposed solutions to worldwide challenges, *Global Viewpoints* volumes offer readers opportunities to enhance their global awareness and their knowledge of cultures worldwide.

Introduction

> *"A nation needs strength to attain and defend its freedom. This strength only comes from courage born of conviction."*
>
> *—Viktor Yushchenko, Acceptance Speech,* Profile in Courage *Award Ceremony, John F. Kennedy Presidential Library & Museum, April 5, 2005*

While campaigning to become president of Ukraine in September 2004, banker and economist Viktor Yushchenko fell critically ill. Doctors in Ukraine were initially unable to diagnose what was wrong with Yushchenko, who was the de facto leader of a moderate, pro-democracy political coalition known as "Our Ukraine." He had to be flown to Vienna, Austria, to a hospital that specializes in intestinal and stomach disorders. Once there, physicians made a startling discovery: Yushchenko had been poisoned with the toxic chemical dioxin. Yushchenko nearly died and had to undergo painful treatments in order to recover. He was also left with severe scars on his face from ingesting the poison. The presidential candidate and his supporters believed that the assassination attempt was carried out by political opponents, led by pro-Russian prime minister Viktor Yanukovych.

Ukraine is a nation of 46 million people in Eastern Europe, bordered by the Black Sea, Poland, Belarus, Hungary, Moldova, Romania, Slovakia, and Russia. It has been ruled at varying times by Poland, the Ottoman Empire, Turkey, and Russia. Ukraine was briefly independent after World War I from 1917 to 1920, before the Soviet Union gained control over the region. The Soviets attempted to suppress the Ukrainian language and culture and allowed little political or economic freedom. Millions of Ukrainians were deported to work camps or forcibly resettled in remote areas of the Soviet Union. Meanwhile, large numbers of Russians were resettled in Ukraine so that by the time of the 2004 balloting, approximately 18 percent of the population was Russian.

Ukraine became independent in 1991, after the end of the Cold War. Leonid Kravchuk was elected the country's first post–Cold War president, followed by Leonid Kuchma in 1994. Although Ukraine's constitution created a democratic system of government, Kuchma concentrated power in the office of the presidency, suppressed the media, and appointed cronies and friends to positions of power. Pro-democracy groups also charged that his regime manipulated elections and engaged in voter intimidation and fraud in his reelection in 1999. Unable to seek a third term in 2004, Kuchma threw his support to Prime Minister Yanukovych.

The election campaign was bitter and hotly contested. Yanukovych was the candidate of the Party of Regions, which was pro-Kuchma and supported closer political and economic ties with Russia. Yushchenko's supporters sought democratic reforms and generally endorsed a closer relationship between Ukraine and Western Europe and the United States. Despite the continuing effects of his poisoning, Yushchenko kept campaigning vigorously and garnered considerable public support. In his acceptance speech for the Profile in Courage Award in 2005, he described his reasons for continuing the campaign: "A patriot of Ukraine, I sought the presidency because I was anguished by poverty, repressed freedom of speech, corruption. . . . I could not calmly watch as the hopes of her citizens were replaced by disillusion, as millions of people were forced to look for work abroad, as oligarchic clans stole the national wealth."

If no candidate secures more than 50 percent of the vote in the initial round of presidential elections in Ukraine, a second round is held. In the initial balloting on October 31,

2004, Yushchenko received 39.9 percent of the vote, while Yanukovych gained 39.26 percent (the rest was divided between more than a dozen other candidates). A second round of voting was held on November 21, and Yushchenko received 46.61 percent, while Yanukovych got 49.46. Yanukovych was subsequently declared the winner. Both domestic and foreign election observers were critical of both rounds of voting because of irregularities and fraud. For instance, in some regions that supported Yanukovych, voter turnout was more than 110 percent of the registered voters. Richard Lugar, a U.S. senator and chairman of the Senate Committee on Foreign Relations, was an observer of the polling; he declared in a November 22, 2004, statement from Kiev that "a concerted and forceful program of election day fraud and abuse was enacted with either the leadership or cooperation of governmental authorities." The United States, the European Union, and a number of other governments announced that they would not recognize the results of the election because of the interference. Meanwhile, Russia, Belarus, and a number of other regional states, including Kazakhstan, Kyrgyzstan, and Uzbekistan supported Yanukovych.

Yushchenko and his supporters launched an official protest of the results to the Ukrainian election commission and the country's court system. In addition, protests spread rapidly across the country. In the capital of Kiev, more than five hundred thousand gathered to protest the results. Yushchenko's supporters adopted orange as their color, and the period came to be known as the "Orange Revolution." On December 3, Ukraine's supreme court declared the results of the November balloting to be null and void and ordered a new runoff election.

A third round of balloting was conducted on December 26. There were domestic and international election observers throughout the country. They contended that the elections were free and fair. When the results came in, Yushchenko won the polling with 51.99 percent of the vote to 44.2 percent for his opponent. Yanukovych protested these results, but the election commission and the courts confirmed Yushchenko's victory in January 2005. He was sworn in as Ukraine's third president on January 23 in what was widely heralded as a victory for democracy. U.S. White House spokesperson Scott McClellan, quoted in a November 6, 2004, *Time* article, declared that the "Orange Revolution was a powerful example of democracy around the world."

After entering office, Yushchenko pursued economic reforms and closer relations with the West. However, the coalition that brought him to power soon fragmented into a number of smaller political parties and groupings. The economic crisis that began in 2008 seriously damaged the Ukrainian economy and undermined public confidence in the president. He placed fifth in his reelection bid in 2010. His former opponent Yanukovych ran a centrist campaign in which he pledged to maintain ties with the West and to undertake economic reforms. He placed first in the initial round of balloting on January 17, 2010, with 35.32 percent of the vote. He also won the runoff election on February 7, with 48.95 percent to his opponent's 45.47 percent. Ukrainian scholar and political commentator Vadim Karasev stated in the February 9, 2010, *Wall Street Journal* that Yanukovych's victory was due to his understanding "that a dictatorial style is no longer permissible in Ukraine. The Orange Revolution made him a politician."

Since the end of the Cold War, democracy has become increasingly common as a system of government around the globe. However, a number of regimes continue to resist domestic and international pressures to democratize. Meanwhile, efforts to promote democracy have met with mixed success. A variety of impediments, both within and outside of countries, continues to hinder and frustrate democracy advocates. Nonetheless, some successes have occurred and many states have made the transition to democracy. The viewpoints in this volume examine a range of issues and controversies surrounding the spread and maintenance of democracy around the world. The authors explore four main points: how governments either promote or resist democracy; what government means for equality; the relationship between democracy and economics; and, finally, the nexus between democracy and international relations. Despite successes, democracy remains fragile and in need of constant attention in order to thrive and spread.

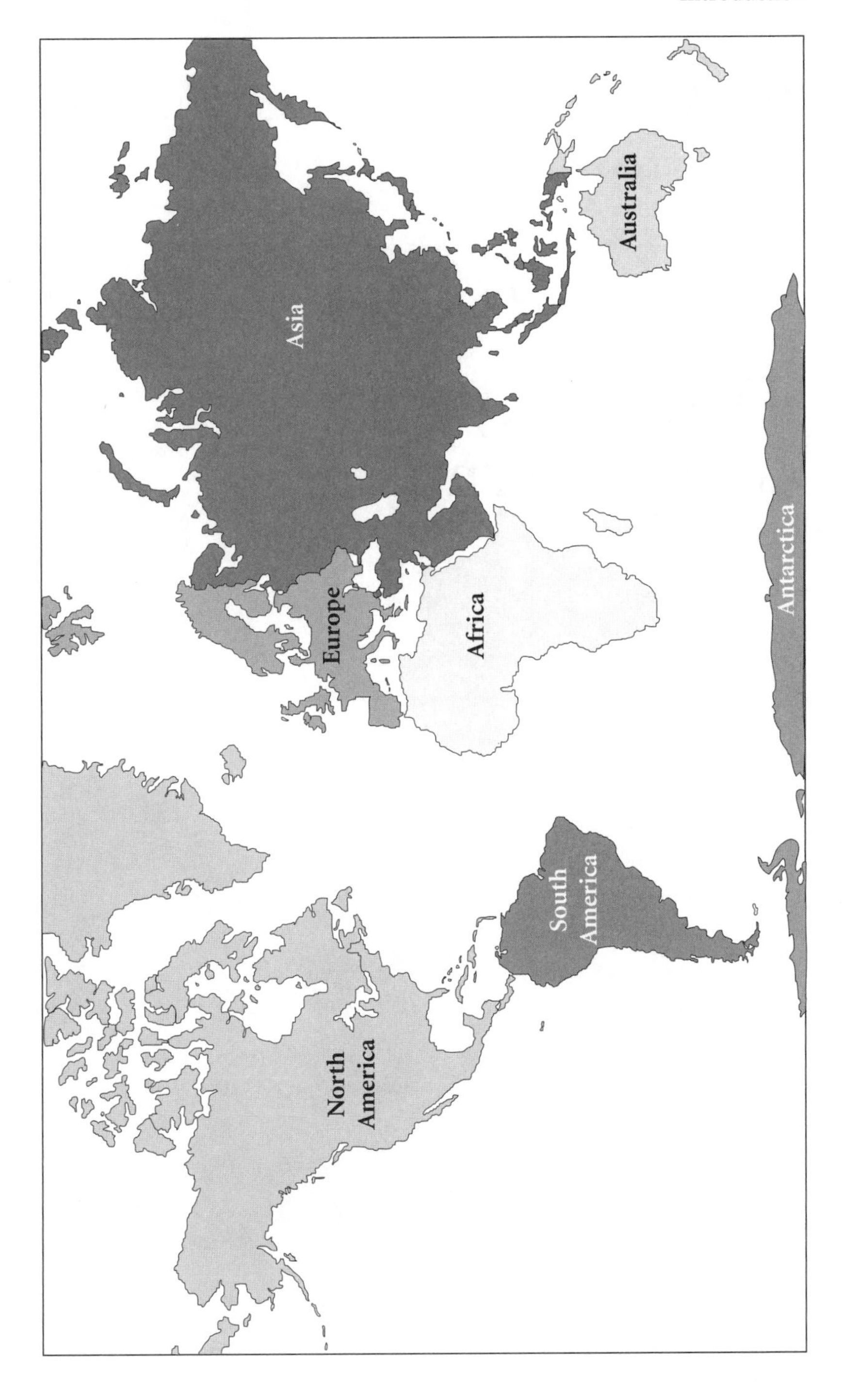
Asia
Australia
Europe
Africa
Antarctica
North America
South America

Chapter 1

Democracy and Government

VIEWPOINT 1

Spain and South Korea Have Significant Challenges in Their Transitions to Full Democracies

Gregory F. Treverton and Spencer Kim

In the following viewpoint, the authors assert that Spain and South Korea provide examples for how states that had repressive regimes can transition to full democracies. However, once democracy is established the country's foreign policy may not always be closely aligned with traditional allies such as the United States. Gregory F. Treverton was a vice chair of the National Intelligence Council and is currently the associate dean at the Pardee RAND Graduate School. Spencer Kim is the cofounder of the Pacific Century Institute and chairman of the CBOL Corporation, an aerospace company.

As you read, consider the following questions:

1. What Spanish leader pledged to withdraw that country's troops from Iraq?
2. The election of what leader in South Korea ended the period of the "three Kims?"
3. What other Asian country does the viewpoint assert has become a full democracy?

Gregory F. Treverton and Spencer Kim, "Snatching Defeat from the Jaws of Victory," RAND Corporation, May 13, 2004. Republished with permission of RAND Corporation, conveyed through Copyright Clearance Center, Inc.

From South Korea to Spain, real democracy is breaking out. Yet for too many voices in the world's preeminent democracy, the United States, that seems like bad news, not good.

Sure, some of the immediate consequences are awkward. Spain is pulling its troops out of Iraq, and South Korea is pursuing an increasingly independent line on a range of issues from North Korea to the presence of American forces in Korea. In Oscar Wilde's line, when the gods wish to punish us, they grant us our wishes; any parent who has wished for his toddlers to grow up knows the wisdom of that line.

Yet the wish for democracy is still the right one. Events in both countries are, in the longer sweep on history, cause for celebration, not moaning.

Spain has been for several decades a member of NATO, and its democracy is a mature one.

Take Spain. At NATO's inception more than a half century ago, France proposed three categories of members, from full ones to those from whom the alliance only needed real estate for bases. France was trying to smuggle in its colonies, and the

United States opposed the idea; Robert Lovett, the undersecretary of state—grade inflation had not yet arrived in Washington, creating deputy secretaries—derided the idea as "resident members, non-resident members and summer privileges."

The idea died, but what is interesting is that Spain under Francisco Franco was such a pariah that it was not even a candidate for summer privileges. Instead, the United States had to make a bilateral agreement to base submarines and aircraft in Spain. Spain's desperation for any international seal of legitimacy produced one of the more memorable guidance cables: Spain's negotiating party in Washington was told to "bargain hard, and if you come up with nothing, sign it."

Now, Spain has been for several decades a member of NATO, and its democracy is a mature one. Its voters have "thrown the rascals" out several times, most recently returning the socialists to power. Coming hard on the heels of the terrorist railroad bombing in Madrid, Americans were tempted to see the election, and incoming Prime Minister José Luis Rodríguez Zapatero's promise to withdraw Spanish troops from Iraq, as electoral cowardice, as an attempt to make a separate peace in the war on terror.

The outcome, however, is better interpreted through Tip O'Neill's maxim that "all politics is local." Loose talk of old and new Europe notwithstanding, the war in Iraq was as unpopular in Spain as anywhere in old Europe, and former Prime Minister José María Aznar deserves credit for the courage of his convictions in sending Spanish troops to Iraq in the first place. When the governing conservatives looked like they were trying [to] point the finger for the Madrid attacks at the Basque separatists, ETA, that smacked of convenient deception to many Spaniards. The attack had few of ETA's trademarks, and when al Qaeda was implicated, voters vented their wrath on Aznar and the conservatives.

Spain and Democratic Challenges

Spain, which has enjoyed democratic rule only since 1977, joined the European Community in 1986. Public security has been marred by the nearly 50-year terrorist campaign of the Basque separatist movement ETA [a terrorist group that has operated on the Basque regions of Spain and France since 1959], which has claimed more than 800 lives, including a politically motivated killing during the 2008 elections.

Heritage Foundation, "Spain,"
2010 Index of Economic Freedom, *2010. www.heritage.org.*

With regard to South Korea, the election of Roh Moo-hyun in 2002 produced hand-wringing in the United States, for the election seem[ed] to bode for difficult times in U.S.-Korean relations. That commentary was wrong then, and similar concerns about recent turns in Korean politics are also off the mark. Roh's election marked the beginning of the end for Korea's regional, personality-driven and corrupt brand of democracy. He lost in his native but conservative southeast, as he had in earlier tries for a parliamentary seat, but won in other regions around the country. Korea's election was cause for congratulations, for Koreans themselves but also for those Americans, missionaries and others, who went to Korea at the turn of [the] last century to introduce American values, especially democracy.

Roh's election was notable for continuity, with the voters opting for the governing party, not swinging to the other extreme. It was also the opportunity for a real changing of the guard. It put an end to the era of the "three Kims"—three men well into their 70s, including the previous president, Kim

Dae-jung, who have dominated Korean politics for a generation. Roh came to office less burdened by the lifetime of deals, compromises and secret money that hung over all his predecessors, even Kim, his immediate predecessor and Nobel Prize winner.

Korea's election was cause for congratulations, for Koreans themselves but also for those Americans, missionaries and others, who went to Korea at the turn of [the] last century to introduce American values, especially democracy.

Only time will tell whether the endemic corruption in Korea's politics can be changed, but recent events suggest that voters may have had enough. The opposition trumped up, then passed, the beginning impeachment proceedings against the president. It was business as usual in Korean politics. Rather, it was business that had been usual. Given the chance to speak on the matter in parliamentary elections several weeks after the impeachment, Korean voters overwhelmingly reject the opposition party, giving Roh a wide margin of support. The impeachment proceedings are likely to be quietly reversed.

What a far cry from South Korea's past, when Roh's pre-[de]cessors became president, if not through the raw power of the military, then through elaborate deals among factions and politicians. South Korea had what political scientists would call "tutelary democracy," with the military performing the tutelage. Both the presidential and the parliamentary elections have seen what is probably better described as rising national pride than anti-Americanism. In that perspective, the alliance to the United States looks very asymmetrical, more appropriate to the 1950s than now. An American still would command Korean forces in wartime, and the Status of Forces Agreement for U.S. troops seems not the equal of those the United States has with other nations, Japan in particular. And the war in Iraq was as unpopular in South Korea as in Spain.

Both Roh and Rodriguez Zapatero now have popular mandates to pursue policies that will provoke discomfort in Washington. In a similar way, now that Taiwan has made the transition from crony, quasi-democracy of the sort South Korea also had, to become a full-fledged democracy, it has acquired more legitimacy. It becomes harder, for good or ill, for the United States to pressure it not to opt for independence.

Yet the discomfort is the fruit of success. One can only hope that eventually China itself will come to see the virtues of real democracy. In the meantime, politics in Spain, South Korea, Taiwan and other countries are rollicking, more than faintly populist, open yet unpredictable—in short, a lot like America's politics. Wishes do come true.

Viewpoint 2

Colombia's Democratization Process Is Hindered by Anti-Narcotics Efforts

Héctor Mondragón

In this viewpoint, Héctor Mondragón explores the ways in which U.S.-supported efforts to suppress the drug trade have undermined Colombian democracy. The cornerstone of the U.S. initiative is "Plan Colombia," which provides funding for counter-narcotics efforts and anti-guerilla campaigns. Despite billions in aid, the author contends that drug lords are more powerful than ever. Nonetheless, a civil democracy movement has emerged that has rejected the violence of guerilla groups and drug traffickers. Mondragón has been a Colombian human rights activist for more than thirty-five years.

As you read, consider the following questions:

1. How much has the United States spent on "Plan Colombia," including expenditures by the U.S. Agency for International Development (USAID)?
2. How much has the Colombian stock exchange increased in value since the 2003 invasion of Iraq?
3. How many trade unionists have been killed in Colombia, according to the viewpoint?

Héctor Mondragón, "Democracy and Plan Colombia," *NACLA Report on the Americas*, vol. 40, no. 1, January–February 2007, pp. 42–44.

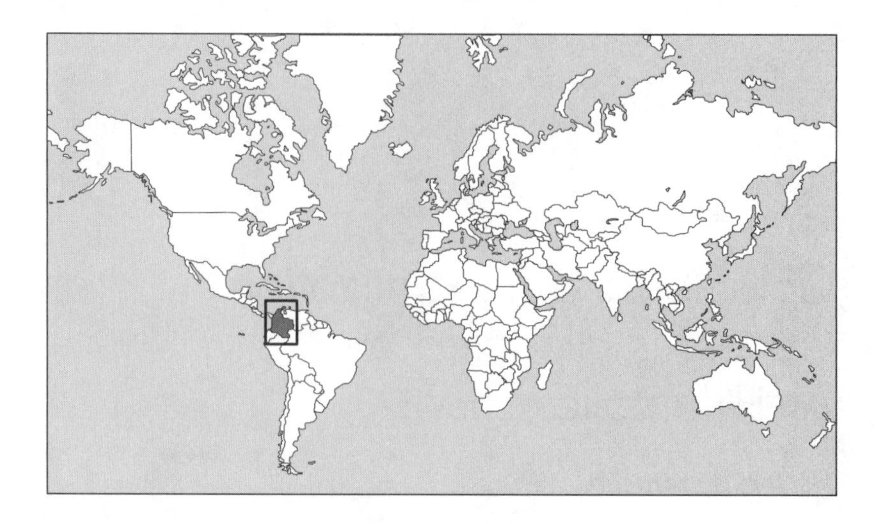

President George W. Bush has asked the American people to "be patient" so that Iraq can become like Colombia—so that the Iraqis can defeat terrorism and establish a stable democracy like the one Washington has nurtured in Colombia. I would like to comment on this nightmare.

Plan Colombia

Plan Colombia, a "pro-democracy" aid package provided by the United States to Colombia, was established in 1999. Its primary stated objective was to end drug trafficking in Colombia. Later on, it was discovered that the plan had the further objective of defeating the guerrilla movement, though that component of the plan was never acknowledged by Washington while Bill Clinton was in office. It was, however, made explicit in subsequent versions of the plan devised by George W. Bush's administration, which identified its principal objective as combating "narco-terrorism," thus conflating the drug war with the anti-guerilla struggle. Furthermore, the Bush government has proposed that the plan combat any other threat to the security of the Colombian state, a proposal that has since been repeated in a State Department document. Obviously, these "other threats" to Colombian security do not refer to extraterrestrials, but to forces like the [Hugo] Chávez government in Venezuela and the indigenous mobilizations in Ecuador—forces that represent anti-neoliberal, anti-imperial changes in South America by way of democratic elections and popular mobilization.

Washington has now spent $4.7 billion on Plan Colombia, and if you include the expenditures of the U.S. Agency for International Development (USAID) in that total, it reaches $7.7 billion. But despite this investment, the U.S.-supported government of Álvaro Uribe [president of Colombia from 2002–2010] has defeated neither the drug traffickers nor the guerrilla movement. To the contrary, the plan's only success has been to guarantee a majority to the parties that supported Uribe in the congressional elections of March 2006 and to guarantee Uribe's own re-election last May [2006].

When Uribe was first elected, his primary campaign promise had been to defeat the guerrillas, and to accomplish this, he instituted a one-time war tax. In his campaign for re-election, he proposed a second "one-time" war tax. The reality is that, far from being defeated, the guerrilla movement in Colombia is today much stronger than when Uribe began his presidency. The guerillas had been hard hit in the last year of the [Andrés] Pastrana government and during Uribe's first year, in part thanks to U.S. technical assistance to the Colombian air force that allowed it to engage in effective anti-guerilla bombing campaigns. The guerrillas had also suffered setbacks due to their own political and strategic errors, many of which negatively—and gravely—affected the civil population.

Nevertheless, the U.S. Southern Command and the Uribe government committed a huge military error known as Plan Patriota, which called for the Colombian armed forces to surround and annihilate the guerrillas in their interior strongholds. But these were locations the guerrillas knew well and where they enjoyed solid popular support, allowing them to soundly defeat the military. Today the guerrillas—especially the FARC—have gained political momentum after having launched an effective counteroffensive. Over the past year the Colombian military's losses in the civil war have considerably surpassed those of the U.S. military in Iraq. The departments of Putumayo and Caquetá have been paralyzed for well over six months, and in many areas of Colombia the army cannot guarantee anyone's safety. Yet despite failing to fulfill his main electoral promise, Uribe still managed to be re-elected. How was this possible? To paraphrase Bill Clinton: It was the economy, stupid.

Colombia's Economy

Like many other areas in the world, Colombia is experiencing a post-Iraq-invasion economic boom. But Colombia's boom may be the least sustainable of them all. Stock exchange values have increased 1,100%, meaning prices have multiplied 11 times. This has not occurred anywhere else since the 1920s, simply because no other country would allow it. Any other national bank or federal reserve system would intervene to curb such inflation, knowing that such rapid unchecked increases in value—which are not the result of growth but of pure speculation—will eventually cause a terrible recession. In Colombia this has not only been allowed, but actually encouraged through specific economic measures. For example, the Colombian state buys its own treasury bonds. It takes the money from its left pocket and lends it to its right pocket, and whereas a moment ago it had only four dollars, it now has eight—four dollars plus a certificate proving it has borrowed another four! So, Colombia receives billions of dollars from the United States as part of Plan Colombia, and the Colombian government then lends the money back to itself. It plays the same game with its public health and pension funds. What's going to happen when the government has to pay this money back?

But this doesn't explain the whole story of Colombia's spectacular growth. There is a much more important explanation: the agreement with the paramilitaries. Many have criticized this agreement, arguing that it amounts to an amnesty for crimes against humanity. But all of this discussion has obscured the economic essence of the agreement, which is to allow the legalization of billions of paramilitary narco-dollars. The paramilitaries finance not only their operations, but also their lifestyles with the country's largest drug-trafficking operations.

Since negotiations between Uribe and the paramilitaries began, billions of dollars and euros in drug profits have entered Colombia. Throughout 2003, 2004 and the beginning of 2005, moreover, the paramilitaries exported a huge quantity of the cocaine they had stockpiled, knowing that anything sold prior to the amnesty would be pardoned under the peace agreement. This is the true cause of the enormous wave of speculation—a sea of illicit funds entering Colombia. And like an emperor of ancient Rome, Uribe was able to provide the populace with "bread and circuses" prior to the presidential elections of May 2006. Was Washington aware of this? Of course it was.

Never before have drug traffickers had so much power in Colombia. Today they have penetrated the stock market, laundered their drug money in the form of treasury bonds and gained a foothold in the electoral process.

Colombia's Drug Trade

What is the primary objective of Plan Colombia? Never before have drug traffickers had so much power in Colombia. Today they have penetrated the stock market, laundered their drug money in the form of treasury bonds and gained a foothold in the electoral process. And although those in Uribe's party who have been publicly identified as drug lords were purged,

The False Promise of Plan Colombia

The money sent down from Washington represents only 13.7% of the total costs of the armed forces and the police.... Also, it's false ... to say that Plan Colombia covers "social expenditures," when in reality not one U.S. cent is spent for that purpose.

Jorge Enrique Robledo, "Understanding Plan Colombia," Canada-Colombia Project, April 3, 2009. http://canadacolombiaproject.blogspot.com.

they created their own parallel pro-Uribe parties and have gotten themselves elected to Congress. This is not to say anything of those drug lords who have not been publicly identified and who remain on Uribe's party's lists.

In the past, drug traffickers financed electoral campaigns from the shadows, financing publicity and paying for hotels and travel. This was a relatively small-scale operation. Today, however, they openly finance entire electoral campaigns. The government's own statistics acknowledge that in 2005, $3 billion flowed through Colombia, with no record of how the money entered the country. No one planted money seeds and grew the $3 billion; this is just a portion of the billions of dollars and euros that the paramilitaries have laundered. Why does Washington, with its moral crusade, the War on Drugs, permit this? Because Colombia serves as its base for attacking the democratic processes taking place in neighboring countries.

This is the reality of U.S. intervention in Colombia. Colombia is becoming an eternal battleground, in order to secure the country as a base of operations for controlling Ecuador, Venezuela and possibly even Peru, Brazil and Bolivia.

They say, "Have patience with Colombia; we're heading to Venezuela and Ecuador! Be patient with Iraq; we're on our way to Iran."

In Colombia we are used to the fabrication of news that prevents us from seeing the reality that Uribe's government reaps a harvest of terror; of 60 years of violence; of the killing of 4,000 trade unionists; of the destruction of workers' rights; of the displacement of three million peasants from their land—and of transnational capital, which finds abundant cheap labor now that its trade unions have been violently destroyed.

Today, [drug dealers] . . . openly finance entire electoral campaigns. The government's own statistics acknowledge that in 2005, $3 billion flowed through Colombia.

In Colombia, however, there is also a democratic civil resistance that rejects the guerrillas' methods and that is often, in fact, victimized by the guerrillas. It proposes a different country—one not ruled by drug barons, where food is secure and where the social movements that have resisted decades of terror have the political weight they deserve. Before paramilitary narco-dollars arrived, this civil resistance was able to elect the mayor of Bogota and defeat a referendum in which Uribe sought to change the constitution to nullify our democratic rights. It has organized general strikes in December 2002 and October 2004; massive indigenous marches called "mingas"; and a popular consultation against the free trade agreement in indigenous regions, in which more than 86 percent of the population voted.

Every day those of us in social movements risk our lives to change Colombia so that our country will stop moving against the grain of the rest of Latin America. Every day we risk our lives so that Colombia can be united with Venezuela and Ecuador, with what the MST (Movimento dos Trabalhadores

Rurais Sem Terra) [Landless Workers' Movement] is building in Brazil, with what the Uruguayans are doing, with what our people are doing these days in Los Angeles. The future of our country is in the balance.

Viewpoint 3

Democracy in Thailand Is Increasingly Under Strain by Internal Forces

Tim Meisburger

In the following viewpoint, Tim Meisburger argues that although Thailand was seen as a model for democracy in Southeast Asia, internal strife has undermined its democratic foundations. Ironically, efforts to strengthen the rule of law have weakened democracy by undermining the political legitimacy of elections and political parties. According to the author, what the country most needs is a decentralization of its political organs and structures. Meisburger serves as the regional director for elections and political processes for the Asia Foundation in Thailand.

As you read, consider the following questions:

1. When did Thailand create a new constitution in an effort to bolster democracy?
2. What was the main mistake made by Thaksin Shinawatra and the Thai Rak Thai party in the 2001 election?
3. What does the viewpoint contend were the three main faults of the 2007 Thai constitution?

As red-shirted protesters continue to block access to the Government House, just as their yellow-shirted foes did a few months ago [in 2008], one wonders where democracy is

Tim Meisburger, "Whither Democracy in Thailand?" *In Asia: Weekly Insight and Features from Asia*, April 8, 2009.

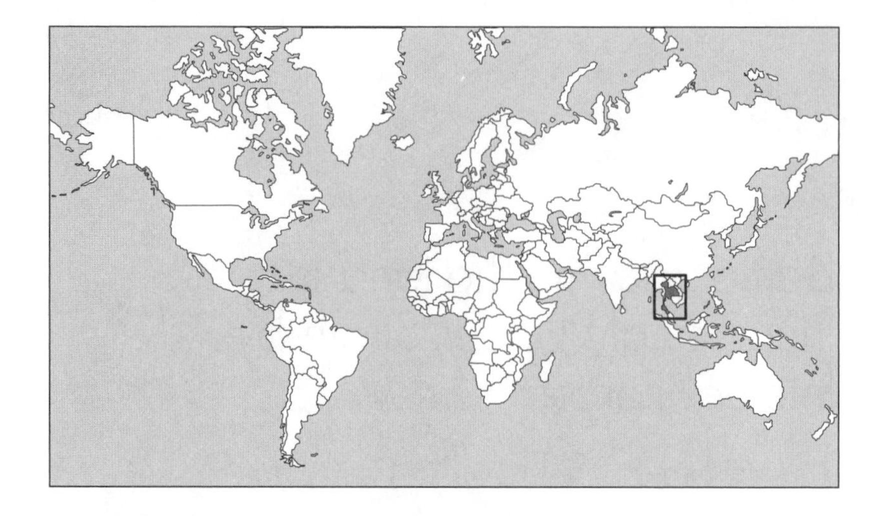

headed in Thailand. A dozen years ago, Thailand drafted a constitution through a participatory process seen as a model for other emerging democracies. Thailand was a rising star, the standard for democratic development that other Asian nations sought to emulate. Now, 12 years later, Thailand's democracy looks tarnished and tattered.

Thailand's Transition to Democracy

After suffering for decades with weak coalition governments, weak protection of human rights, and changes of government through military coups, Thailand crafted a new constitution in 1997 that was intended to usher in a new era of democratic government. It would strengthen the executive branch of government while providing stronger checks and balances on its authority, strengthen rights protection for ordinary people, and remove forever the threat of a military takeover of civilian government. Unfortunately, since then the stronger executive branch has easily overcome the checks and balances incorporated in the constitution, successive governments have trampled on the rights of the people, and the military has seized power through a coup and has rewritten the constitution. How did it all go wrong, and what can Thailand's people do to regain their place as the foremost democracy in Southeast Asia?

Over the past eight years, the country has become increasingly polarized, and its institutions politicized. The rapid period of polarization began when Thaksin Shinawatra and his Thai Rak Thai party ran for office in 2001 on a populist platform that appealed directly to the urban poor and rural masses, bypassing completely traditional power brokers in the military, bureaucracy, and business. This created an opportunity to define society in a different way: us versus them, poor against rich, the weak but virtuous standing up to crooked but powerful vested interests. These splits may have been more perception than reality to begin with, but perception is powerful, and over time can create its own reality.

Unfortunately, since [the drafting of the constitution in 1997] the stronger executive branch has easily overcome the checks and balances incorporated in the constitution, [and] successive governments have trampled on the rights of the people.

In recent years, color has also contributed to the polarization of society. Yellow shirts were once worn on Mondays to show love of the King, but now to wear a yellow shirt is to clearly declare one's political allegiance, just as wearing a red shirt places one in the opposing camp. Inevitably caught in the middle is the monarchy itself, with yellow-shirts claiming that anyone who does not agree with their position is against the monarchy, and red-shirts responding that the yellow-shirts show disrespect to the monarchy by using the King's color for their own political purposes. Color has become a code that allows complex situations to be simplified; it's black or white; he's red and she's yellow; that province is red and that one yellow, etc.

The institutions of state, including the independent institutions established under the 1997 constitution, are increasingly viewed as heavily politicized, which contributes to the corresponding impression of a decrease in rule of law in Thailand. During Thaksin's time as prime minister, the courts and the election commission were believed by many to be under his control or influence, but since the coup these institutions are generally perceived (at least by Thaksin's supporters) to be biased in favor of his political opponents; the People's Alliance for Democracy, the military, and the Democrat Party.

The 2007 Constitution

Although many people believe the 2007 Thai constitution is in some ways better than the 1997 constitution that it replaced, it lacks democratic legitimacy and weakens democracy for a number of reasons. First, it was drafted by a team appointed by the military junta that seized power in 2006. And in addition to provisions designed to advance the junta's political agenda, it includes a blanket amnesty for the coup makers. Second, it strengthens unelected institutions, and changes the Senate from a wholly elected to a partially appointed body, weakening accountability. Third, it was enacted through a referendum process fraught with fraud, in which voters' only choice was to either approve the junta's constitution or allow the junta to revise one of Thailand's previous constitutions.

Unfortunately the current Democrat-led coalition government, which assumed office through normal parliamentary procedures, also lacks democratic legitimacy, as it came to power not through popular elections but because of the court-ordered dissolution of other political parties and the banning of those parties' most popular politicians. Although a provision allowing the dissolution of political parties was included in the 1997 constitution, the laws that allow banning politicians were drafted by the junta, presumably with the intention of suppressing their political opponents.

Timeline of Contemporary Democracy in Thailand

1997: New, democratic constitution drafted.

2001: Thaksin Shinawatra elected prime minister.

2005: Thaksin reelected.

2006: Thaksin is removed from office during military coup.

2007: New, military-backed constitution is approved in referendum; elections are held, and Samak Sundaravej becomes prime minister.

2008: Former prime minister Thakasin flees Thailand following corruption charges. The allegations lead to widespread protests. Samak is dismissed from office and replaced first by Somchai Wongsawat, and then by Abhisit Vejjajiva, who becomes the third prime minister in three months.

2009: Pro-Thaksin demonstrations spread throughout the country and martial law is declared. Unrest causes cancellation of the Association of Southeast Asian Nations summit.

2010: Anti-government protestors hold repeated demonstrations in Bangkok between March and May and paralyze the Thai capital. A government-sponsored deal over early elections fails to end the protests. Clashes between demonstrators and security forces result in the death of anti-government leader Maj. Gen. Khattiya Sawasdiphol along with more than twenty others. In May, security forces storm the main headquarters of the protestors.

Compiled by editor.

Dissolving political parties and banning many politicians for the crimes of a few is in legal terms called "collective punishment." It punishes the innocent politicians barred from office, but also punishes the voters who are denied the political representation they voted for. Voters will understand if a corrupt politician is found guilty of a crime and removed from office for cause, but when their representative is removed by the court for no cause, and replaced with a representative from a party they did not vote for, voters will understandably perceive the courts as unjust or biased and the new representative appointed by the court as illegitimate.

Although many people believe the 2007 Thai constitution is in some ways better than the 1997 constitution that it replaced, it lacks democratic legitimacy and weakens democracy.

The Poor

Although the political conflict in Thailand has been personalized to a large extent, there are real issues that underlie the political divide. Prior to Thaksin's election, many rural and urban poor people felt exploited and believed the government was too focused on the interests of a middle-class and wealthy Bangkok-based academic and commercial elite. After Thaksin's election there was a marked shift in policy, and people in the city felt slighted. They resented being forced to pay for his populist programs aimed at rural areas and complained of a tyranny of the majority.

One means to reduce this tension could be political decentralization. If people in a local area have control over, and pay for, their own services, there will be no reason for conflict with other areas, while democracy and accountability will be enhanced. Political decentralization might also help resolve the separatist conflict in the south.

Another way to reduce tension and improve democratic representation would be to allow people to vote where they live. Currently, many people who live in Bangkok are counted for representation in their home village or town, meaning that those areas are over-represented in national government, while Bangkok is under-represented. If representation and voting were based on where people actually live, Bangkok people would not feel under-represented, and everyone would enjoy better representation and improved political accountability.

VIEWPOINT 4

Democratization in the Middle East Is Hindered by Conflict

Jim Lobe

In the following viewpoint, Jim Lobe contends that U.S. efforts to promote democracy in the Middle East have been undermined by continuing conflict in the region and missteps by the administration of former president George W. Bush. The author notes that even former allies of the United States such as Saudi Arabia and Israel have pursued their own policies in order to resolve disputes in the region. Lobe is a journalist and the Washington bureau chief for Inter Press Service news agency.

As you read, consider the following questions:

1. What does the viewpoint argue was one of the successes of U.S. policy in the Middle East?
2. Who is the most important Arab ally of the United States in the region, according to the viewpoint?
3. According to Lobe, what country has played a significant role in easing tensions in the region in areas such as Lebanon?

More than five years after invading Iraq as a first step towards "transforming" the Middle East, the administra-

tion of U.S. President George W. Bush seems to have lost its footing in the region.

The talk of "democratizing" the Middle East has almost entirely disappeared from the administration's rhetoric. Washington has had to sacrifice whatever pressure it had been willing to exert on "friendly authoritarians" before to bolster its rule against popular sentiment, which has become considerably more hostile toward the U.S. than before the invasion.

Impact of the 2006 Israeli-Hezbollah Conflict

Similarly, its plan after the 2006 Israel-Hezbollah war to forge a de facto coalition between the Jewish state and those same "moderate" authoritarians against the threat posed by Iran, Syria and their allies in the Levant has also failed.

Not only has the administration repeatedly refused to pay the Arabs' price for such an arrangement—putting serious pressure on Israel to reach a peace accord with a unified Palestinian government based largely on a return to the 1967 borders—but the assumption that the Arab Gulf states, in particular, would welcome and support an eventual military confrontation between Washington and Tehran [the capital of Iran] has also proved illusory.

The surge's strategic goal—national reconciliation between the key sectarian and ethnic groups in Iraq—remains elusive, as evidenced by the latest impasse between Arabs and Kurds over Kirkuk.

The one area in which Washington has made some progress has been in Iraq where sectarian violence has fallen sharply over the past 18 months [in 2007–2008] in good part as a result of more successful counterinsurgency tactics pursued by General David Petraeus during the "surge" of some 30,000 additional troops.

But the surge's strategic goal—national reconciliation between the key sectarian and ethnic groups in Iraq—remains elusive, as evidenced by the latest impasse between Arabs and Kurds over Kirkuk and the certainty that long-promised regional elections will be delayed until next year.

Even Petraeus continues to warn that the security gains made since the surge got under way in February 2007 remain fragile and could be reversed in the absence of significant political progress.

Washington's continuing preoccupation with Iraq—as well as its growing concern about Afghanistan and Pakistan—has effectively undermined its larger transformational ambitions in the Arab world, in particular, leaving local powers to work out their own arrangements with each other, even in ways that make the administration uneasy or even angry.

"The hard-line, confrontational policy the United States has embraced under the Bush administration has inadvertently demonstrated the limits of U.S. power," according to a recent paper published by the Carnegie Endowment for International Peace. "The rejection of diplomacy has reduced the United States to a condition of self-inflicted powerlessness regarding many problems."

"The vacuum is being filled in part by U.S. adversaries—Iran, Syria, Hamas and Hezbollah—and in part by friendly Arab regimes, which seek to find a way forward in situations where U.S. policy has contributed to stalemate," according to the report, entitled *The New Arab Diplomacy: Not with the U.S. and Not Against the U.S.*, by Carnegie fellows Marina Ottaway and Mohammed Herzallah.

This is particularly notable with respect to the gradual détente between Iran—Washington's main regional nemesis since the Iraq war—and Saudi Arabia, traditionally Washington's most important Gulf ally.

The Role of Saudi Arabia

That process, which has included two visits to Saudi Arabia by Iranian President Mahmoud Ahmadinejad, as well as his unprecedented participation at a Gulf Cooperation Council summit, is credited in major part to Saudi King Abdullah, who has made little secret of his aim—contrary to that of the administration's hawks—to reduce Sunni-Shia tensions that came to the fore after the Israel-Hezbollah war.

Abdullah, who shocked the U.S. when he negotiated the ill-fated unity government between Hamas and Fatah in early 2007, also worked with Iran to calm sectarian tensions in Lebanon that year despite his steadfast backing for Washington's efforts to isolate Syrian President Bashir al-Assad.

Similarly, Qatar, which hosts a huge U.S. air base, has played a leading role in reducing tensions in the region, most notably by negotiating a political settlement to the long-

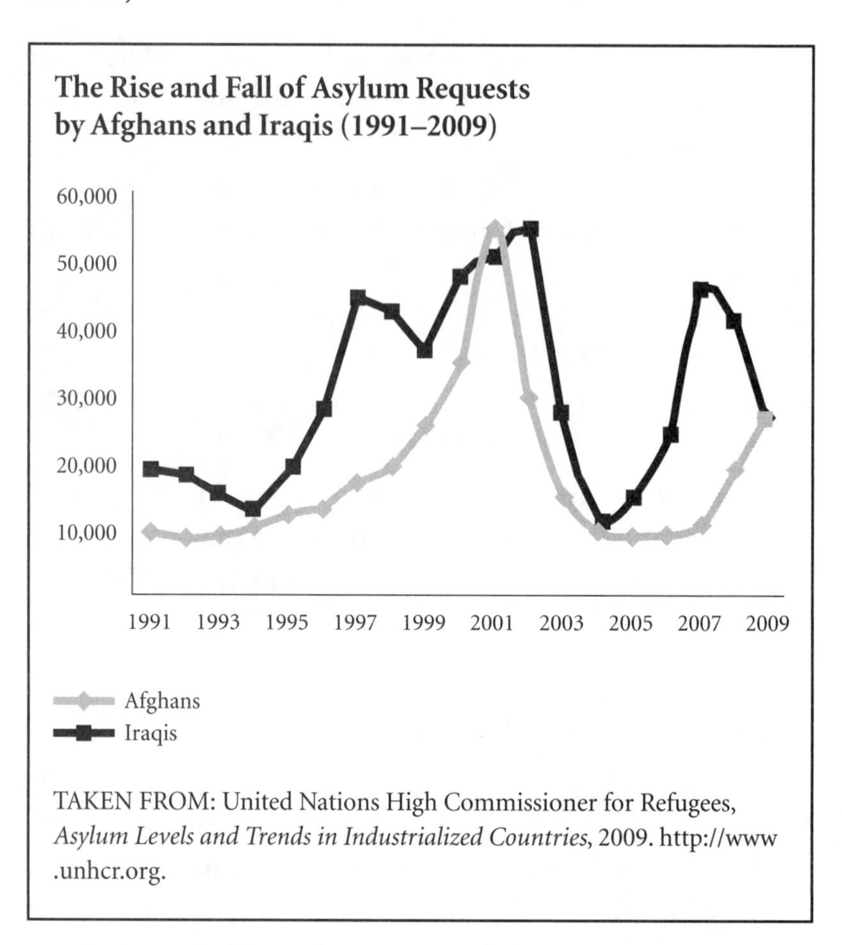

TAKEN FROM: United Nations High Commissioner for Refugees, *Asylum Levels and Trends in Industrialized Countries*, 2009. http://www.unhcr.org.

running standoff in Lebanon in May that resulted in the U.S.-backed government of Prime Minister Fouad Siniora.

Washington's closest ally in the region, Israel, has declared at least partial independence from the Bush administration, notably by using third parties in the region to engage adversaries whom Washington persists in trying to isolate.

While U.S. Secretary of State Condoleezza Rice endorsed the accord during a visit to Beirut in June, most analysts here and in the region depicted the result as a serious blow to Washington's regional position.

"Many essentially friendly countries are openly willing to pursue policies the United States disapproves of, presenting Washington with a 'fait accompli' and the choice of either openly criticizing the action of its so-called allies or grudgingly tolerating it," the Carnegie report said. "The United States has little leverage over the policies of even friendly countries."

While the new report focuses primarily on Arab diplomacy, it does mention that even Washington's closest ally in the region, Israel, has declared at least partial independence from the Bush administration, notably by using third parties in the region to engage adversaries whom Washington persists in trying to isolate.

Thus, through Egypt, Israel has negotiated what appears to be an increasingly effective ceasefire with Hamas, and it may soon conclude a prisoner exchange with the Islamist group, just as it did—again in the face of Washington's clear disapproval—with Hezbollah last month [July 2008].

The government of Prime Minister Ehud Olmert has also been pursuing increasingly intensive, Turkish-mediated negotiations with Syria that have, according to the Israeli press, acquired the backing of the Jewish state's entire security establishment.

Syria's Role

Damascus has been the target of unceasing efforts by the White House, in particular, to isolate and punish neoconservative hawk Elliott Abrams, who assumed the top Middle East post in the National Security Council on the eve of the Iraq invasion. Indeed, it was only two years ago, during the opening days of the Israel-Hezbollah war, that Abrams suggested that Israel carry the fight into Syrian territory.

Now, according to Israeli press reports, the two countries are within reach of a final peace accord, which could come as early as the next round of proximity talks in September.

Damascus, however, is insisting that Washington give its explicit blessing to the agreement, a blessing that, given Abrams's enduring influence—despite the wishes of the State Department and the Pentagon—most analysts believe will likely await the arrival of a new administration next year.

While such "negative power" remains a very real factor as Bush's tenure winds down, it appears increasingly detached both from any practicable strategic vision and from the wishes and desires of key U.S. allies in the region.

VIEWPOINT 5

Malaysia's Democracy Suffers from Abuses of Power

Andrew Aeria

Andrew Aeria contends in this viewpoint that Malaysia's government uses a variety of tactics including voter fraud, censorship, and repression to prevent true democracy. He asserts that the government also utilizes state media to undermine its opponents and critics. Despite elections, the same trends continue, and prodemocracy activists face various forms of intimidation including arrest and imprisonment. Aeria is a member of the executive committee of Aliran, a Malaysian human rights organization that supports democratization.

As you read, consider the following questions:

1. Despite laws calling for local elections, what has been the only village to hold elections for chief?
2. According to the viewpoint, how many people have died in police custody since 2003?
3. What are the names of the newspapers that the viewpoint asserts are targets of government censorship?

March [2008] heralded a new dawn for democracy [in Malaysia] after all those dark years of repression, frustration and dashed hopes. After nearly five decades of nationhood, we had had enough. We were tired of Umno/BN's

Andrew Aeria, "Our Broken Democracy," Aliran, March 24, 2009. Reproduced by permission.

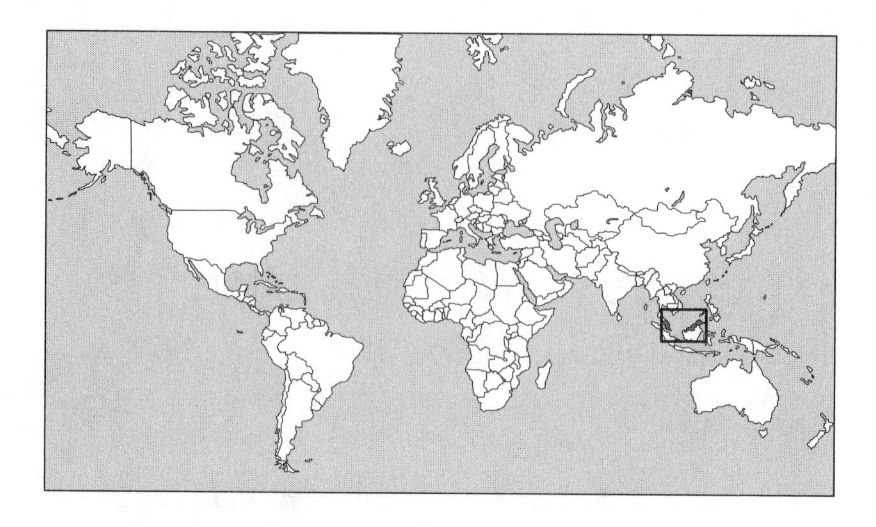

[United Malays National Organization/Barisan Nasional's] feudal, non-transparent, non-accountable, and crass attitude towards governance. For far too long, the country had endured nauseating corruption, civil service inefficiency, police impunity, elite hypocrisy, political detentions, religious intolerance, racism and Umno-putera greed.

Even longtime Umno/BN supporters disillusioned with the sheer levels of corruption, lack of leadership and drift within the coalition were not unhappy. For them, it was good that the governing coalition was delivered a big slap. Many hoped that Umno/BN would learn, change their bad habits and renew themselves. Others hoped that PR [Pakatan Rakyat, a political party] would reform and renew the five states they now governed.

In our heads and hearts, the delicious thought swirled, "Yes! There is hope now for Malaysia!" We wanted change! A progressive and democratic society! Among others, we wanted a new political culture 'where feudalism, corruption, nepotism, hypocrisy and double standards are done away with once and for all'. We wanted democratic and governance reforms. We wanted responsive and responsible electoral democracy. We wanted improvement to our human rights and

2008 Elections in Malaysia

In the 2008 Malaysian balloting, the ruling coalition, the National Front, retained its majority in the parliament, but suffered its worst electoral showing since 1969 as the opposition coalition of political parties, the People's Front, had its best showing in history. Opposition critics charged that the election was marred by fraud.

Coalition	Percentage of Votes	Seats in Parliament	Gain or Loss of Seats
National Front	50.27	140	Lost 58 seats
People's Front	46.75	82	Gained 62 seats

TAKEN FROM: Compiled by editor.

civil liberties. We wanted judicial independence and the rule of law strengthened. We wanted an independent and responsible media.

In other words, we wanted our 'broken democracy' fixed.

Yet, one year on, much of the abuse and nonsense still exists. Indeed, as the French put it so exquisitely, 'plus ça change, plus c'est la même chose' or 'the more things change, the more they remain the same'.

March [2008] heralded a new dawn for democracy after all those dark years of repression, frustration and dashed hopes.

Electoral Democracy

We all remember the indelible ink fiasco [the Election Commission cancelled the use of indelible ink to mark voters' fingers in the March 8, 2008, election]. Additionally, we have long had serious reservations about 'phantom voters', postal votes, the mainstream media's propaganda, the persistent abuse of government machinery, instant minor rural projects, and gifts and cash handouts to voters and journalists during elections.

In 2004, an extensive two-year nationwide study . . . found that "the Malaysian electoral system and the process of legitimation (sic) coming from it is increasingly under strain". Lacking credibility, the professional response from the Election Commission (EC) would have been to improve its act.

We have long had serious reservations about 'phantom voters', postal votes, the mainstream media's propaganda, the persistent abuse of government machinery, instant minor rural projects, and gifts and cash handouts to voters and journalists during elections.

But what have they done since March 2008? Nothing! Thus, electoral irregularities continue. Supposedly, the EC cannot act since policing electoral irregularities is not their responsibility. And yet, when it suits their political masters, the EC can act with great creativity even vetoing the right of Speakers to declare vacant a legislative seat as it did in Perak [a state in Malaysia] recently.

Then, there is the contemptible behaviour of the four Aduns in Perak who thought nothing of betraying the electorate by defecting (the Umno guy Nasaruddin defected twice!). The honourable thing would have been to consult their constituents, explain their reasons for wanting to defect and obtain consent. But no. They simply defected. And, some suspect, were rewarded financially for doing so.

In the process, they deposed a legitimate government via dubious means and precipitated a constitutional mess. In retaliation, Speaker V. Sivakumar suspended the 'new BN Menteri Besar' Zambry Kadir and his whole 'Exco' from the legislative assembly. Perak politics is now a farcical circus. Anwar Ibrahim has since revealed in parliament that many other PR

MPs [members of Parliament] and Aduns have also been approached to defect. He talked of bribes and blackmail, of ringgit [the Malaysian currency] millions, bullets and kidnapping threats.

Local Government

And what about local government elections? In February 2005, Lim Guan Eng speaking to DAP [Democratic Action Party] leaders said, "We must restore local government elections for the sake of democracy, good governance, rule of law, accountability and transparency." The DAP and PKR [People's Justice Party] 2008 general election manifestos both listed local government elections as a key promise.

Today, only Gunung Rapat New Village in Perak has balloted to elect their village chief. Nobody else has done so, nor are they encouraged. Instead, every PR state government has given excuses (yawn!) to avoid holding local government elections. PR's attitude here only imitates the BN's gravy train of rewarding grubby party cronies with local government appointments instead of allowing the rakyat to freely choose their local government representatives.

Additionally, instead of fulfilling their 2008 election manifesto promises to ensure better living standards, provide a healthy environment for the future generation, and to preserve forests and protect urban green lungs, the DAP/PR Penang state government is reluctant to stop dangerous hillslope development projects despite having the power to do so. Notwithstanding pressure from the Tanjong Bungah Residents' Association, the state government is hesitant about protecting life and property. It's also ambivalent about securing water catchment resources.

Housing developers continue violating federal government hillslope guidelines on steep and dangerous (i.e., Class 3 and 4) hillslopes in Tanjong Bungah and Batu Ferringhi. Ignoring the risks to and fears of residents, the Penang government mumbles incoherently about 'not wanting to be sued'.

Despite our hopes, electoral democracy remains 'broken'.

In effect, DAP Penang has compromised and become very business-friendly since winning government. It seems afraid to upset developers. Is this because DAP Penang has quietly received donations from developers? What value then should voters place on DAP manifesto promises? Strikingly, the PKR/PR government in Selangor has been unafraid to ban all hillslope developments. Why the contradiction?

Despite our hopes, electoral democracy remains 'broken'.

Human Rights

Who can forget the cruel Internal Security Act (ISA) being used against MP Teresa Kok, Raja Petra Kamarudin and journalist Tan Hoon Cheng in September 2008? As well, the five Hindraf [Hindu Rights Action Force] leaders—M Manoharan, P Uthayakumar, V Ganabatirau, R Kengadharan and K Vasantha Kumar—remain icons of resistance to the heinous injustice of detention without trial. But for how long more? How many more must march shackled in the footsteps of the thousands since 1948 before this wicked law is repealed? Presently 'at least 50 people are detained indefinitely without charge or trial under the ISA'.

Hindraf remains outlawed. One cannot assemble or speak or identify with the Hindu Rights Action Force. Neither can one wear a Hindraf T-shirt and go visit the PM during his open house Hari Raya lunch as happened last October [2008]. That apparently was a 'disturbance' and seemingly 'against the law'.

Neither can one cycle peacefully to parliament in a Jaringan Rakyat Tertindas (Jerit) campaign. When Jerit activists did so over a fortnight last December to highlight the plight of poor workers, food shortages, non-affordable housing, minimum wage demands, opposition to health services privatisation and the repeal of the ISA, they were harassed by police all the way. Throughout the campaign, some 200 detentions were recorded, including about 50 arrests. Apparently, cycling for a cause is not allowed. 'Thugs' burnt a few of their bicycles. If only the police showed similar enthusiasm in tackling crime and arresting real criminals, what a safe place Malaysia would be.

The Role of the Security Forces

The police resist reforms. A Royal Commission to Enhance the Operation and Management of the Royal Malaysian Police was set up in February 2004 over public concerns of human rights violations, abuse of power, corruption, and ineffective or unresponsive work practices within the police force. In May 2006, 125 recommendations were made, key being the formation of an Independent Police Complaints and Misconduct Commission (IPCMC). Unfortunately, it remains a non-starter. Instead, a toothless version of the IPCMC bill (called SIAP) will soon be tabled in parliament despite it not commanding public confidence.

And what of those thousands of migrants and refugees who come to Malaysia to seek work or to escape violence and political persecution? Instead of receiving succour, nearly all tell ghastly tales of being horribly abused and exploited. Migrant workers are treated like commodities, 'bought and sold like fish and vegetables'.

They are harassed and extorted . . . , their passports confiscated. Trafficked like cattle (with women forced into the sex trade by the criminal underworld), they are squeezed for every last drop of their blood. [Human/migrant rights organization] Tenaganita recently alleged that Burmese Rohingyas, some even holding UNHCR [United Nations High Commissioner for Refugees] documents, are "arrested, jailed and deported, but since they are stateless they are taken to the Thai border and often sold to Thai traffickers".

US Senate Foreign Relations Committee staff "are said to be reviewing reports of extortion and human trafficking from Burmese and other migrants in Malaysia, allegedly at the hands of Malaysia government officials". Remember plantation worker R Ganesh who starved to death and maid Nirmala Bonat who was hideously tortured? They have gone now but others still suffer sadistic treatment. In 'a monstrous act of barbarism', a hundred persons were discovered forced into a 1,000 sq ft [square foot] shop-house unit only to be released when their manual strength is required for work we are too lazy or too dainty to do ourselves'.

Legal or otherwise, are these workers and refugees not 'entitled to the same basic human rights as anyone else'? Who protects them?

Despite our hopes, human rights remain 'broken'.

The quality of our judiciary is mediocre. It continues to underperform.

Judicial Independence and Rule of Law

In 2007, the infamous Lingam Tapes revealed a can of worms about judicial fixing. It sparked a firestorm of indignation. Demands for judicial reform led to the adoption of the Judicial Appointments Commission (JAC) bill. Among its key aims are to maintain judicial independence; guarantee transparency and meaningful consultation in judicial appointments; allow stakeholder representation; ensure accountability and outline selection and promotion criteria of judges.

But the JAC does not impress or inspire public confidence. The Bar Council says the JAC falls short and does not even meet its own professed aims. Put differently, judicial independence will remain compromised for the foreseeable future.

The quality of our judiciary is mediocre. It continues to underperform. And how to erase such perceptions when the Altantuya Shaariibuu murder trial leaves so many questions unanswered and so many crucial persons not summoned to testify? The judge and prosecution team mysteriously got changed earlier on. Statutory declarations are disregarded and evidence ignored during the trial. Certain lines of questioning are blocked. Bala goes missing, Razak Baginda walks free, and the two suspects remain masked in court raising suspicions about their true identity. Many bloggers suggest it's all a stitch-up job.

And what tragedy befell Kugan Ananthan? Healthy when taken into police custody, he was soon dead after 'a drink of water'. He became another statistic, adding to the 1,535 that have died in custody since 2003. Then, there are those alleged 'armed robbers' who get killed 'after they first shoot at the police'; the latest being the six 'gold robbers' in Kulim, Kedah. Whether suspected 'car thief' or 'bank robbers', are they not innocent until proven guilty? Should they not be tried in court? Instead the Home Minister and police view them as 'criminals'. Whatever happened to the rule of law? Or are we being vulgarly ruled by law?

Selective prosecution continues. Consider the Malaysian Anti-Corruption Commission (MACC). Despite media hype, it's a sick joke. Little has changed. Instead of acting on numerous reports of alleged serious corruption cases, the MACC goes after minnows and PKR. It wants to investigate Speaker V Sivakumar for alleged abuse of power. It wants to charge the Selangor Menteri Besar over a luxury car and a few cows!

No action on the BN's alleged multimillion ringgit efforts to bribe and bully PKR lawmakers to defect. No action on the Sabah or Sarawak Chief Ministers both of whom are exorbitantly rich, their wealth acquired during their terms in office. Nothing on the allegations of corruption during the Kuala Terengganu by-election, Umno money politics or the $14.39

billion Port Klang Free Zone scandal. No investigation of Samy Vellu's multimillion ringgit corporate shenanigans involving MIED [Maju Institute of Education Development] and AMIST [Asian Institute of Medicine, Science and Technology University]. And certainly no case on DPM Najib despite allegations surrounding submarines and Sukhoi aircraft.

And then there is Bukit Antarabangsa. Another major hillslope collapse and more deaths [in December 2008]. God and the rain have been blamed (again). The tragedy likely occurred because the local authority and developers cut corners and closed one eye to wrongdoing. Just like Highland Towers [the apartments collapsed in December 1993]. No respect for the 'rule of law'. But hey, this is Malaysia. So, nobody is going to get prosecuted and certainly not the developer. Instead, Elizabeth Wong, who stood up against greedy condo developers by pushing through a PKR state government ban on hillslope development in Selangor, is wickedly targeted and hounded from office.

Despite our hopes, judicial independence and rule of law remains 'broken'.

The Media

Our government-owned and politically linked mainstream media (MSM) are, to put it mildly, trashy and compromised. A scrutiny of the MSM during March 2008, the Permatang Pauh and Kuala Terengganu by-elections will confirm this. A quick perusal of the Centre for Independent Journalism (CIJ) Web site [www.cijmalaysia.org/] will inform readers about the MSM's backward state. Sometimes it's hard not to compare our sycophantic MSM with previous lowlife media like Soviet TV news and newspapers *Pravda* (lit. The Truth) and *Izvestia* (lit. The News).

This was seen again recently in the way the MSM covered the story involving the perverse distribution of surreptitiously taken private photos of [Malaysian politician and human rights activist] Elizabeth Wong. Here, our MSM's sinister game of gutter journalism and gutter politics revealed itself. *Malay Mail* led the charge on 16 February [2009] when it splashed an unrelated photo of a barebacked Formula One model on its front page next to bold headlines, "Fury over bedroom invasion".

Prominent blogger Anil Netto noted, 'apart from the juxtapositioning of an unrelated picture next to a sensationalist story, the choice of front-page story is revealing'. Further stories of 'moral outrage' from Umno Youth president wannabe Khir Toyo (of all people!) followed and were highlighted by the MSM. They played up the photos and cast aspersions on Elizabeth's character when the crime was its distribution.

Conscientious readers were rightfully disgusted and incensed. Elizabeth Wong has since resigned and Malaysian politics has lost a hardworking lawmaker. Indeed, the old Russian saying about *Pravda* and *Izvestia* best reflects the state of our MSM today. "v Pravde net izvestiy, v Izvestiyakh net pravdy" (In the Truth there is no news, and in the News there is no truth).

Suara Keadilan and *Harakah* are now being targeted. The Home Ministry has seized thousands of copies of both newspapers this year. These confiscations continue despite Malaysia pledging in 2006 to 'promote a free media, including in cyberspace'. In the recently concluded UN Human Rights Council [Universal] Periodic Review meeting in Geneva, Amnesty International noted that 'Malaysia has failed to uphold these pledges to respect human rights, including its commitment to promote a free media, particularly the Internet. Bloggers have been charged under the vaguely worded provisions of the Sedition Act'. A view Raja Petra, Sheikh Kickdefella and others would heartily agree.

Thus, despite our hopes, our media remains 'broken'.

Hopes Dashed

Our hopes for a better society have been dashed yet again, and this time not only by BN but also by PR. Both coalitions have underperformed since March 2008. Frustratingly, despite a looming recession, they are squabbling. They are wasting time and resources. Their conflicts are risking our rice bowls. There is scant realisation that with government power comes heavy responsibility for the larger interests of the nation. It seems the rakyat's interests do not matter. Instead, personal and party interests are being put ahead of the rakyat's deepening economic woes. Consequently, there is currently a lot of political instability and uncertainty. This is bad for business and wearisome for ordinary folks desperate to make ends meet. 'The political machinations since the beginning of this year have done little but undermine the will and the fundamental democratic rights of the Malaysian people'. There is already a deepening lack of confidence in the country's institutions. At this rate, Malaysia runs the real risk of going down the road to becoming a failed state.

Ghana's Elections Provide Lessons for Democratization

Stephan Gyasi Jr.

In the following viewpoint, Stephan Gyasi Jr. analyzes the 2008 Ghanaian elections. The balloting was judged to be free and fair by both domestic and international observers. The author details how many incumbents lost their seats as a reflection of general voter dissatisfaction with current conditions in the country. He asserts that the results are reflective of the maturity of democracy in Ghana and serve as a model for other countries in the region. Gyasi is a Ghanaian journalist and writer.

As you read, consider the following questions:

1. Who were the two previously democratically elected presidents of Ghana?
2. Which Ghanaian political party ruled the country from 2000 to 2008, as stated in the viewpoint?
3. According to Gyasi, how many seats did the National Patriotic Party (NPP) win in the 2004 Central Region provincial elections?

Many elections in Africa in recent years have been harrowing affairs, marred by malpractice, violence and death. Not so in Ghana, whose independence in 1957 opened the floodgates to African liberation from colonial rule. That,

Stephan Gyasi Jr., "Lessons in Democracy (Ghana)," *New African*, vol. 24, no. 4, January 2009.

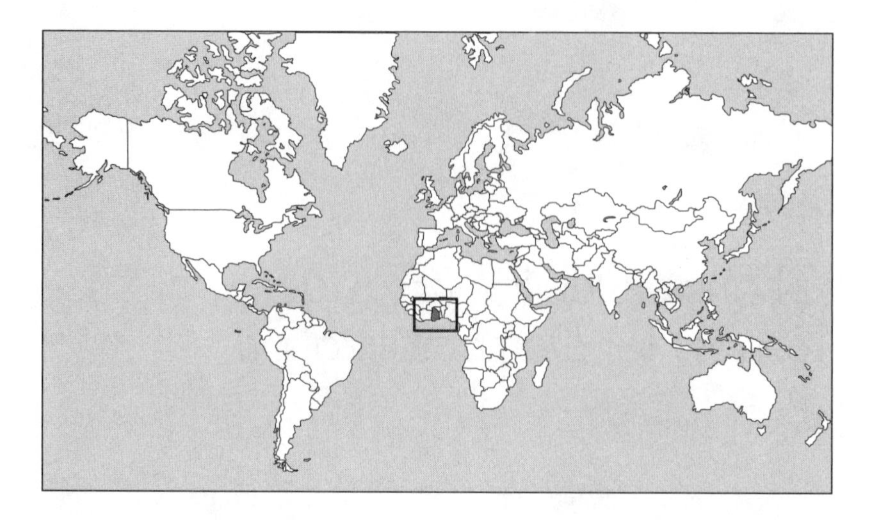

enough, is not to say that reckless statements about "going the Kenyan way" had not been made in Ghana by some party supporters in the months and weeks leading to the elections.

Kenya exploded after its elections in December 2007, in which the opposition accused the government of fiddling with the figures and eventually rigging the elections.

The violence, which went on for two months, claimed over 1,000 lives. But not so in Ghana, giving the many international election observers who flocked to the country cause to salute Ghanaians and describe the electoral process as "generally peaceful, orderly, free and fair."

Kenya exploded after its elections in 2007. . . . The violence, which went on for two months, claimed over 1,000 lives.

Ghana's Democratization

The African Union observer mission, headed by the former OAU [Organisation of African Unity] secretary general, Dr Salim Ahmed Salim, praised Ghana's election as a "consolidation of democracy" and "a good example" to West Africa and Africa as a whole.

After several military coups since 1966, Ghana went the democratic way in 1992 and has since held four peaceful elections in 1996, 2000, 2004 and now 2008. During the same period, two democratically elected presidents finishing their constitutionally mandated two terms (of 8 years each)—Jerry Rawlings and John Kufuor—have peacefully stepped aside to be replaced by their elected successors.

If all goes well during the runoff on 28 December, the democratic lessons from Ghana will resonate throughout Africa, a continent that has seen some ugly elections in the recent past.

A Draw in the First Round

The elections, especially the presidential, were expected to be a breathtaking encounter between the ruling New Patriotic Party (NPP) and the opposition National Democratic Congress (NDC) and it did not disappoint!

It ended up throwing the poll into a second round scheduled for 28 December after neither the NPP's Nana Addo Dankwa Akufo-Addo nor the NDC's Professor John Evans Atta Mills garnered the constitutionally required "50%+1" of the valid votes cast to win on the first ballot.

Akufo-Addo polled 4,159,439 valid votes or 49.13%, while Mills, running for president for the third time, got 4,056,634 votes or 47.92%. It was that close. Their nearest rival, the CPP [Convention People's Party] candidate Paa Kwesi Nduom, who came third, was left far behind with a miserly 113,494 votes or 1.34%.

The results, from a national voter turnout of 70%, show that claims by both parties ahead of elections that they were heading for a "one-touch" victory did not resonate with the electorate. The pattern of the election clearly shows that Ghanaian democracy is maturing, and voters have started looking beyond the bread and butter issues normally used by politicians in their campaigns, to critically analyse the politicians' planned policy directions and how practical their plans are for improving the lives of the people.

"The results . . . reflect a referendum on the performance of the incumbent. It is the people's verdict, and I think it's a good challenge in our democracy. It is an indication of the people's maturity."

Following this logic, it is no surprise that the ruling NPP appears to have been stung by "the sin of incumbency", leading to its relatively poor showing at the polls. In the parliamentary election, for example, the NPP lost its majority in parliament where it had 128 of the 230 seats. It won only 112 seats in this election to the NDC's 113, a remarkable performance by the opposition party that had suffered a crippling defeat in 2004 when it won only 92 seats.

Analysts were quick to point out that "this is a punishment vote against the ruling party" whose economic performance, and the scandals and behaviour of some high-up government officials had attracted public disapproval in recent months.

"The results," says the political analyst and University of Ghana lecturer Kwame Karikari, "reflect a referendum on the performance of the incumbent. It is the people's verdict, and I think it's a good challenge in our democracy. It is an indication of the people's maturity."

Before declaring the final results, the chairman of the Electoral Commission (EC), Dr Kwadwo Afari-Djan, flanked by other members of the EC, states that there was no constitutional provision that enjoined the commission to declare election results in 72 hours, so the anxiety which according to the media was growing among Ghanaians based on the "delay" in releasing the results was misplaced. However, he praised the media for the comprehensive coverage they had given the polls and also for the neutral stance they had taken in the declaration of the ongoing results.

The NPP, which has ruled the country for the past eight years, failed to clinch the promised "one-touch victory" because there was general voter apathy in the regions where it holds sway. For example, in the Ashanti Region—the NPP's traditional bastion—voter turnout was 62% as against 88.7% in 2004, while the national average in 2008 was 70%.

If the party should win the runoff on 28 December, its strategists will have to quickly find out why thousands of their supporters in the Ashanti Region failed to turn up.

The region is known for its phenomenal voter interest but political analysts say the seeming indifference to this election is a reflection of the complacency that the NPP leadership attached to its campaign in the region.

The party's general secretary, Nana Ohene Ntow, has expressed shock at the turn of events, but has, however, assured the party faithful that victory will be theirs come 28 December.

Contrary to the NPP woes, the opposition NDC appears to have enjoyed massive turnout from its support bases. Its general secretary, Johnson Asiedu Nketia, claimed that the party's "sublime performance" was a strong message to the government that Ghana was not prepared to be left out of the "hurricane of change" blowing across the world, and that the NDC would employ every constitutional means to ensure victory in the second round.

The runoff is reminiscent of the 2000 election where the NPP's John Kufuor garnered 48.4% of the votes while the then vice president, John [Evans] Atta Mills, the NDC's candidate, got 44.80%. Mills subsequently lost in the second round to Kufuor, who was supported by the other smaller parties in the runoff.

2008/2009 Presidential Elections in Ghana

In January 2009, in the second round of presidential balloting in Ghana, the two candidates that had the highest votes in from the December polling, Nana Akufo-Addo of the New Patriotic Party and John Atta Mills of the National Democratic Congress, ran against each other in a run-off election. Mills won the second round of balloting.

Candidate	Percentage of Votes	Number of Votes
John Atta Mills	50.23	4,521,032
Nana Akufo-Addo	49.77	4,480,446

TAKEN FROM: Compiled by editor.

The NPP thus believes that history will be repeated on 28 December, but the NDC is convinced that the other parties will rather swing to its side.

This has set the stage for intense lobbying of the smaller parties. Interestingly, the runoff will be decided on a first-past-the-post basis, and the "50%+1" requirement will not apply. Mills has been beaten twice in the past—in 2000 and 2004 by Kufuor, and if he loses again on 28 December, for a third time, he will kiss goodbye forever to his ambitions of becoming president. So he has more to lose than his rival, Akufo-Addo.

Election Day

Queues started forming at polling stations as early as 3 a.m., four full hours before voting started. Voter turnout was just shy of 70%.

The two leading contenders, Akufo-Addo and Mills, were former classmates at the University of Ghana; they are both legal luminaries and played in the university's football team together during their schooldays, but have now found themselves on opposite sides of the political divide.

As part of efforts aimed at safeguarding peace, the media was barred from calling the election in favour of any party before the official announcement by the EC. This, according to the Ghana Journalists Association, was to prevent any situation where a political party might confront the EC with results from a media house. It was also meant to avoid tension brought on by the release of conflicting results.

As the results trickled in from the various constituencies, it became clear that some big names would not be returning to parliament, having been defeated in their respective constituencies. They included the two deputy speakers in the House, Freddie Blay (CPP) and Alhaji Malik Alhassan Yakubu (NDC).

Also defeated (on the NPP side) were Hajia Alima Mahama, minister of women and children's affairs who was touted as vice presidential running mate before she was ditched by Akufo-Addo at the 11th hour; Boniface Abubakar Saddique, minister of water resources, works and housing; Stephen Asamoah Boateng, minister of information and national orientation; Angelina Baiden Amissah, deputy minister of education; and Dr Gladys Ashietey, deputy minister of health.

As the results trickled in from the various constituencies, it became clear that some big names would not be returning to parliament, having been defeated in their respective constituencies.

The NDC equally lost some stalwarts in its strongholds. For example, its incumbent in the Jomoro constituency of the Western Region, Lee Ocran, was resoundingly defeated (by more than 6,500 votes) by Samia Nkrumah, the daughter of Ghana's first president, Dr Kwame Nkrumah, who left her base in Italy to contest for the first time. She won a landslide victory, a mark of the respect her legendary father still holds in those parts.

Samia's campaign had been marked by dirty tricks employed by the NDC party machine on behalf of the 64-year-old Ocran, but Nkrumah's only daughter soldiered on, to emerge as the only representative in parliament of her father's once strong party.

Other defeated NDC stalwarts included the outspoken Dr Ben Kumbour and Mahama Ayariga in the Lawra-Nandom and Bawku Central constituencies respectively. The Builsa South and Chiana-Paga seats held by the NDC also went to the NPP.

But overall, the NPP recorded more casualties in the parliamentary election than the NDC. In Accra, it lost the Ledzokuku and Adenta constituencies, and was defeated in the Mfantsiman West, Cape Coast, Shama, Effutu and Gomoa East constituencies, all in the Central Region. It also lost at Nkawkaw in the Eastern Region, and at Nalerigu-Gambaga, Yendi and Salaga seats in the north.

In the 2004 elections, the NPP won 16 of the 19 seats in the Central Region, the home region of Mills, leaving the NDC with only two seats. In 2008, the NDC did much better, winning 8 seats in the Central Region to the NPP's 11.

In what can be described as a major setback, the first deputy speaker of Parliament, Freddie Blay, a CPP MP [member of Parliament] of long standing, lost his seat in the Ellembelle constituency in the Western Region after his campaign was dogged by controversy which ended in court.

He was accused of "flirting" with the ruling NPP by leaders of the CPP, leading to bad blood between him and the party on whose ticket he had represented the constituency for 12 years. The CPP also lost the Evalue Gwira and Komenda-Edina-Eguafo-Abirem seats to the NPP and NDC respectively.

Elsewhere, the former general secretary of the NPP, Dan Botwe, who was instrumental in Kufuor's two presidential triumphs of 2000 and 2004 but later fell out of favour, won the Okere constituency seat by more than 5,000 votes against his closest rival, George Opare Addo.

The Meaning of the Results

With these developments, it is becoming increasingly clear that Ghanaians now demand greater accountability from their elected representatives. The pattern of voting shows that the idea of "safe seats" is gone forever.

Candidates who were highly tipped to win certain seats have been left counting their losses.

There were a few ugly scenes though. Even before the final results were released by the EC, both the NDC and NPP were accusing each other of trying to rig the polls. In fact, the NDC virtually called the poll in its favour after results from only 42 of the 230 constituencies had been officially declared by the EC.

It is becoming increasingly clear that Ghanaians now demand greater accountability from their elected representatives.

The NDC claimed that statistics in its custody indicated that it had won in more than 100 constituencies. "We know we have won the elections and no amount of underhand acts by the NPP and its surrogates, [would] make us repeat the mistake of 2004," the party said at a hastily convened press conference.

But this was sharply countered by the NPP, which claimed that the NDC was only preparing the grounds for the electorate to reject the results if the official EC tally showed them to have lost in the end.

Security was high at every polling station to ensure that no agent provocateurs brought the credibility of the polls into question.

A joint operation involving the various security agencies under the auspices of the National Elections Security Task Force ensured that Ghana's time-honoured peace and democratic credentials remained untainted during the elections.

The former president, Jerry Rawlings, issued a statement thanking the people for turning out in their numbers to vote, and their exemplary level of comportment during the voting process.

Periodical Bibliography

The following articles have been selected to supplement the diverse views presented in this chapter.

Pranab Bardhan	"India and China: Governance Issues and Development," *Journal of Asian Studies*, May 2009.
Thomas Bierschenk	"Democratization Without Development: Benin 1989–2009," *International Journal of Politics: Culture, & Society*, 2009.
Andrew Lee Butters	"Iraq's Messy Democracy," *Time*, March 15, 2010.
Andrew Coyne and Paul Wells	"Canadian Democracy Is Broken," *Maclean's*, September 18, 2009.
Babak Dehghanpisheh	"Rebirth of a Nation," *Newsweek*, February 26, 2010.
Vuyiswa Joy	"Namibia, After the Elections," *New African*, January 2010.
Lawrence Lessig	"How to Get Our Democracy Back," *Nation*, February 3, 2010.
Philip Levitz and Grigore Pop-Eleches	"Why No Backsliding? The European Union's Impact on Democracy and Governance Before and After Accession," *Comparative Political Studies*, November 30, 2009. http://cps.sagepub.com.
Joshua Muravchik	"The Abandonment of Democracy," *Commentary*, July/August 2009.
Keith Richburg and Reason Wafawarova	"Head to Head: African Democracy," BBC News, October 16, 2008. http://news.bbc.co.uk.
Ming Sing	"Explaining Mass Support for Democracy in Hong Kong," *Democratization*, February 2010.
Claire Spencer	"Middle East: Voting, but for What?" *World Today*, December 2005.

CHAPTER 2

Democracy and Equality

VIEWPOINT 1

Only International Pressure Will Prompt Burma to Democratize

Amitav Acharya

Amitav Acharya argues in the following viewpoint that it is critically important for the international community to promote democracy in Burma (officially the Republic of the Union of Myanmar), which is currently ruled by a military dictatorship. The author briefly focuses on efforts by the regional group, the Association of Southeast Asian Nations (ASEAN), and the obstacles faced by that body including resistance in Burma and an unwillingness by some ASEAN nations to interfere in the domestic politics of a member country. Acharya works for the Institute for Defence and Strategic Studies at the Nanyang Technological University in Singapore.

As you read, consider the following questions:

1. When was the Association of Southeast Asian Nations (ASEAN) founded?
2. Who is the leader of Burma's pro-democracy political party, the National League for Democracy?
3. According to the viewpoint, which ASEAN country adheres to the principle of noninterference because of the potential precedent that intervention could set?

Amitav Acharya, "Democracy in Burma: Does Anybody Really Care?" *YaleGlobal Online*, September 1, 2005.

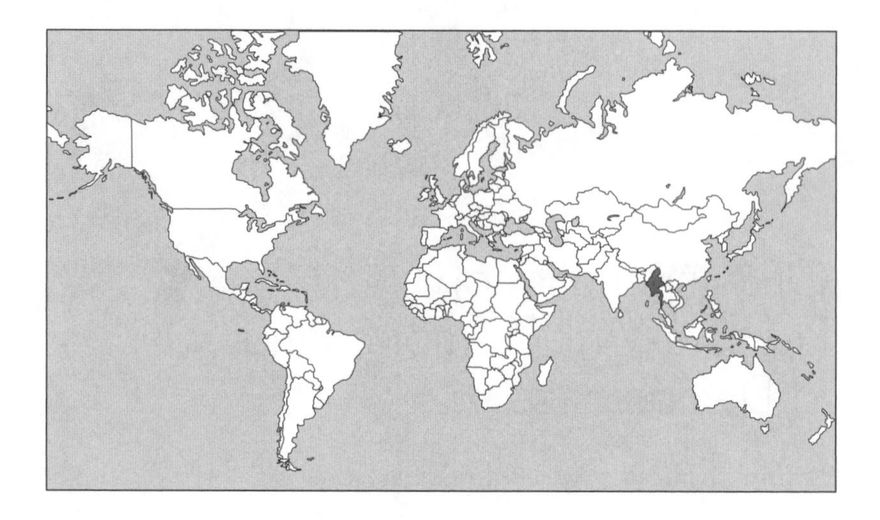

A July 2005 agreement among the members of the Association of Southeast Asian Nations (ASEAN) that Burma [officially the Republic of the Union of Myanmar] would relinquish its turn at the chairmanship has averted a major diplomatic crisis for the organization. Western nations, including the United States [US] and the European Union [EU], who attend the annual ASEAN meetings as "dialogue partners," had threatened to boycott the 2006 meeting if Burma was in the chair.

The Role of ASEAN

Founded in 1967, ASEAN now includes 10 countries of Southeast Asia. Under its rotational leadership, Burma, which joined the group in 1997, was due to assume the chairmanship of its Standing Committee in 2006.

The Western dialogue partners of ASEAN are protesting against continued political repression and human rights abuses by the Burmese regime, which has ruled the country since 1962. The regime has refused to accept the result of the 1990 national election, which was won by the opposition National League for Democracy (NLD). The party leader, Aung San Suu Kyi, has since spent most of her time under detention.

By giving up its claim to lead ASEAN in 2006, the junta managed to take the heat off the question of domestic reform. And ASEAN avoided a Western boycott of its 2006 meeting. But without more focused action by ASEAN and the international community to move Burma towards democracy, the move will be little more than ASEAN's traditional practice of sweeping problems under the carpet.

The discussion in Laos was not about how to improve the political situation in the country. The issue was Burma's leadership, rather than membership in ASEAN. ASEAN has not made Burma's continued membership of the association subject to political reform.

The regime has refused to accept the result of the 1990 national election, which was won by the opposition National League for Democracy.

ASEAN has been reluctant to push Burma towards political reform out of deference to its doctrine of noninterference. The Burmese junta has started drafting a new constitution, due to be completed in 2007, which it says would lead to political liberalization. Presumably, this would make Burma eligible to assume the leadership in ASEAN.

ASEAN members agree and hope that this will be the case. But its Western partners dismiss the constitution-drafting process. Suu Kyi and her party have boycotted the National Convention drafting the constitution, whose delegates were handpicked and tightly controlled by the junta. The [George W.] Bush administration in May 2004 stated that because "Rangoon's constitutional convention has not allowed for substantive dialogue and the full participation of all political groups, including the NLD, it lacks legitimacy." If approved by a popular majority in the electorate in a free and fair referendum—which is by no means guaranteed—the constitution

"Three Monks—Burma," cartoon by Glenn Foden, www.CartoonStock.com. Copyright © Glenn Foden. Reproduction rights obtainable from www.CartoonStock.com.

would still accord the military a privileged position in the political system, including sole claim to the presidency.

ASEAN's role in Burma has been very different from its role in the Cambodia conflict during the 1980s, when it led efforts to find a peaceful settlement to the dispute, which resulted in the Paris Peace Agreement in 1991. That conflict was originally a civil war, although it had been internationalized by Vietnamese intervention and occupation of Cambodia. There has been no outside intervention in Burma, which is one justification for ASEAN's hands-off policy. But Burma has proven to be a major embarrassment for ASEAN.

Approaches to the Burmese Crisis

ASEAN's diplomatic options in dealing with Burma are limited by intramural differences within the grouping over how to deal with the junta. Some members—Indonesia, Malaysia, Philippines, and Singapore—are increasingly concerned about the group's relationship with Western nations, if not its international public reputation per se. Thus, these ASEAN countries want to see the association play a role in nudging the junta to reform. Others, like Vietnam, stick to the principle of noninterference, and are worried about setting a precedent of allowing regionalist pressure for domestic political reform—a precedent that would likely come back to haunt them.

ASEAN's capacity for inducing political reform in Burma is also constrained by the fact that the junta has secured backing from both China and India, its two most powerful neighbors, playing them against one another. Hence, the junta can ignore any demand for political change that ASEAN may bring to bear on it.

China and India are critical to any intervention by the international community in Burma. But is the West really interested in advancing political change in Burma? There is no serious diplomatic effort ongoing today—of the kind one finds in Sri Lanka or Aceh—that might help bring about political reconciliation in Burma. The Bush administration snubbed ASEAN by canceling Secretary of State Condoleezza Rice's attendance at the Vientiane meeting. But this posturing was almost entirely cost-free, thanks to good bilateral relations with key Asian nations, as indicated by a separate Rice stopover in Bangkok before the Vientiane meeting. Diplomatic snubs and economic sanctions are no substitute for a policy of seeking a solution to Burma's political woes.

Burma's strategic location or economic potential may be apparent to India and China, but not to the US. Burma is not regarded by the Bush administration as a terrorist haven, although it claims to side with the US on the war on terror, supposedly against extremist elements among its Rohingya muslim minority. When asked by the author as to why the US is not actively seeking a role in the Burma problem, a senior official in the first Bush administration replied that because there is no significant domestic interest or constituency in the United States pushing for such a role. The administration's democracy-promotion agenda does not extend to Burma, despite the fact that Secretary Rice named Burma as one of six "outposts of tyranny" during her Senate confirmation hearing in January [2005].

Yet, a diplomatic effort backed by the US and involving Burma's giant Asian neighbors would be necessary and timely. Denying Burma the chairmanship of ASEAN is good posturing, but it does not advance the cause of democratic transformation in the country. If the US could engage in six-party negotiations involving China, Japan, Russia, and South Korea to deal with the North Korea problem, why should it not encourage a similar move involving China, India, and ASEAN to deal with the Burma issue?

Diplomatic snubs and economic sanctions are no substitute for a policy of seeking a solution to Burma's political woes.

The Need for International Intervention

The international community needs to prove that while taking a moral high ground on Burma's crisis, it must also offer concrete ideas and approaches to advance the democratization and national reconciliation process beyond the current policy of sanctions and boycott. A necessary step in that direction would be a new diplomatic initiative to persuade the Rangoon regime to broaden the constitution-drafting process—with the participation of freed opposition leaders and a firm timetable for internationally supervised elections. Such an initiative could be spearheaded jointly by ASEAN, China and India, with the backing of the US and the EU and other members of the international community.

Ultimately, ASEAN must come out of its noninterference closet and address the issue head-on. Otherwise, its hands-off approach will continue to cloud its legitimacy and credibility as a regional organization with a mandate for seeking "regional solutions to regional problems."

VIEWPOINT 2

South Africa Must Overcome Institutional Obstacles to Democratic Equality

Burton Joseph

In the following viewpoint, Burton Joseph analyzes the controversy over Jacob Zuma, the president of South Africa. Specifically, the author argues that opponents of Zuma attempted to manipulate state institutions to pursue their political goals. In doing so, they threatened to undermine democracy and equal rights for both Zuma and average South Africans. In the end, Joseph asserts that democratic forces overcame the challenges to equality posed by some political elites. Joseph is a former Fulbright Scholar, and he is currently a contributing editor to the Star, *a South African newspaper.*

As you read, consider the following questions:

1. What was the motivation for Zuma's trial, according to the viewpoint?
2. Who is Zuma's main political rival in South Africa?
3. What groups does the viewpoint contend were the first to rise to the defense of Zuma?

Burton Joseph, "Zuma Saga a Win for Democracy; For Seven Long Years, the ANC President's Human Rights Were Violated but, in the End, Justice Prevailed," *The Star* (South Africa), April 28, 2009, p. 12.

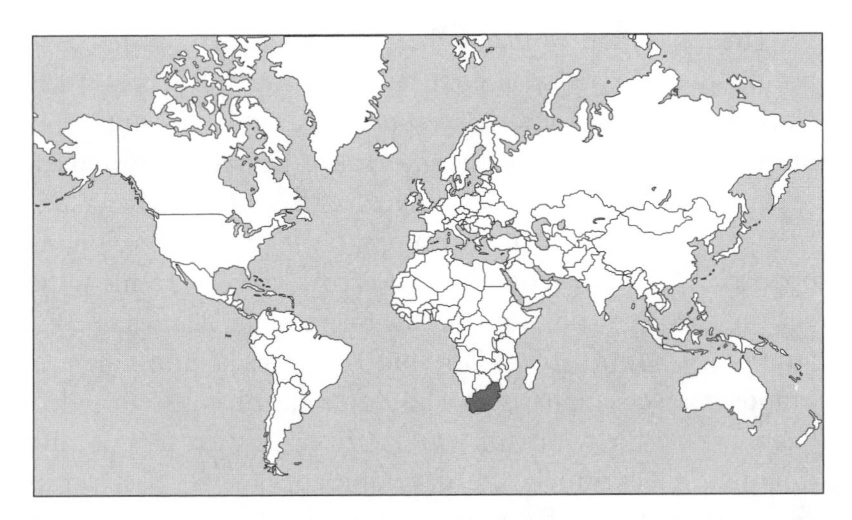

The withdrawal of charges against ANC [African National Congress] president and South African president-elect Jacob Zuma in the Durban High Court [in 2009] marks the end of a very tempestuous period in the country's history and politics.

Issues such as the nature of the state in transition, human rights, grassroots activism, gender politics and the rule of law came to the fore during the saga and produced diverse perspectives, as well as numerous interest groups which attempted to influence the outcome of developments.

The Saga of Zuma

It has become necessary to reflect on this saga which preoccupied us as a nation for more than seven years. The Zuma saga has revealed a peculiar connivance between politicians, public servants and captains of industry in their efforts to discredit political opponents and thwart their ambitions. The edited, taped conversations which were submitted by the Zuma defence team to the National Prosecuting Authority [NPA] implicate key figures who relentlessly pursued their objective for more than seven years.

This revelation confirms the claim by Zuma and his supporters that his trial was politically motivated. It has also left citizens exasperated and has exposed the rapid corruption of our body politic since the attainment of liberation. Moreover, it demonstrates the vulnerability of citizens to the machinations of the state and its functionaries. State persecution, as opposed to the protection it must accord citizens, seems to be equally alive and comes in various forms and disguises in contemporary South Africa. The need for checks and balances cannot be over-emphasised. The Zuma saga has left an indelible mark on the nature of South African politics. It is not my intention to chronicle the developments of the past seven years. Suffice to say that significant interest has been generated in the judicial process, which is good for consolidating democracy.

The findings and recommendations of the Khamphephe commission have effectively sealed the fate of the Scorpions [a multidisciplinary agency disbanded in 2009 that was used to investigate corruption]. What should be interesting to observe over the next few months is the public response to the ANC policy directive for an accelerated transformation of the judiciary.

State persecution, as opposed to the protection it must accord citizens, seems to be equally alive and comes in various forms and disguises in contemporary South Africa. The need for checks and balances cannot be over-emphasised. The Zuma saga has left an indelible mark on the nature of South African politics.

The acknowledgment by the NPA that there was indeed political interference in the prosecution of Zuma ("a compromising of the process", as it euphemistically defines it) gives credibility to the assertion by Zuma that he was a victim of political power play. Such interference has impacted rather divisively on the internal politics of the ANC as activists coalesced around Zuma and [Thabo] Mbeki respectively in the contestation for party leadership. The persistence of the Zuma/Mbeki template within and beyond ANC politics as a result of the acrimonious pre-Polokwane battles must be liquidated quickly and effectively if the party intends to succeed with the implementation of its new policies and the delivery of its election manifesto commitments.

ANC activists who were unable to come to terms with the outcome of the election and the subsequent forced resignation of Mbeki as state president formed the breakaway COPE [Congress of the People] party, ostensibly to protect the values on which our liberation struggle was fought and which underpin our democratic state.

In the process of its formation, the Freedom Charter was invoked to legitimise an undemocratic impulse and which united a myriad of forces arraigned against the ANC, albeit temporarily.

The COPE phenomenon has actually served to resuscitate the ANC in a similar manner to how the formation of the ANC Youth League and the 1949 Programme of Action reversed the fortunes of a stagnant movement. Scores of party members who retired from political activism since the attainment of freedom in 1994 have been drawn back into the fold. Youth participation in politics has increased exponentially, with the ANC visibly experiencing a surge in support.

The assertion by the late ANC Eastern Cape president Reverend James Calata during the 1940s that "Congress is in the hearts [of] the people" reverberates many generations later as young and old are now uniting in defence of the ANC.

The COPE threat to ANC rule has been greatly exaggerated. The fascination with formation is out of proportion to its sustainability, given the basis for its formation, social composition, loose leadership arrangement and internal divisions which have plagued the party since its inception.

> ### Zuma Has Tried to Unite South Africans
>
> [Jacob] Zuma ... committed himself to be a president for everyone by including the two most senior leaders of the Communist Party as well as the leader of the conservative white Afrikaner Party in government....
>
> Both parties deserve our appreciation for accepting the challenge. It is of the utmost importance that pragmatism and not ideology dominates and that all the elements of government set out to work together.
>
> The huge benefit Zuma brings is that he embodies the identification, style and aspirations of the poor and marginalised. The best we all can do for our future is to forget the past, take Zuma at his word and support him fully, irrespective of which political party we may represent.
>
> *Franklin Sonn, "We Must All Back Zuma to Bring Real Change,"* Cape Times *(South Africa), June 3, 2009.*

Lessons from Zuma's Troubles

There are nonetheless important lessons to be learnt from the Zuma saga. To start with, political vigilance is central to the effective transformation of our country.

The workings of this "axis of evil" which sought to direct political developments, and brought the country close to the precipice, have finally been exposed. What made elected representatives succumb to their whims, and what lessons are in this for the new crop of representatives who will assume public office in a few days' time?

It will be their responsibility, and that of relevant institutions, to exercise effective oversight to prevent a recurrence of the abuse of public institutions for factional political battles. Parliament can never be an extension of the executive, in the same manner that its speaker is not just another Cabinet minister. They represent the voice of the people whose human rights they must uncompromisingly defend, at all times.

The erosion of the oversight role and vibrancy of public institutions was counterbalanced by civil society organisations which appeared more alert to this emerging threat to our democracy. It was the trade unionists, Communists and various support groups who initially united in defence of the rights of Zuma. Their tenacity under difficult conditions, and during which time they emphasised political principles and the rule of law, is commendable.

Citizen Participation

Robust political participation by citizens must therefore be encouraged, an aspect which ushers us into the realm of human rights. The constitutional guarantees of equality of dignity and rights of all persons must be upheld.

Those forces which indefatigably defended the human rights of Zuma must be applauded. Such an extraordinary defence of human rights of an individual must be extended to South Africans high and low, given the indivisibility and inalienability of rights of all citizens. South Africa simply cannot afford a passive and depoliticised citizenry as this would create space for the erosion of the values which underpin our fledgling democracy.

The transformation of South Africa has been marked by numerous challenges during the past 15 years. The Zuma saga is one such challenge, which proved to be a stern test for the durability of our public institutions and civic participation. It has accentuated the need for united action and resilience when human rights are under attack and state institutions abused for sectarian political battles.

VIEWPOINT 3

Eastern European Equality Advocates Are Decreasing in Numbers and Efficacy

Agnieszka Graff

Agnieszka Graff contends in the following viewpoint that the public in Eastern Europe no longer trusts the nongovernmental organizations and groups that led the transition to democracy in the region in the later 1980s and early 1990s. Instead, she asserts that competition for resources and the power of the Church have eroded confidence and diminished the effectiveness of these groups. Graff is a writer, human rights activist, and professor in the American Studies Center at the University of Warsaw.

As you read, consider the following questions:

1. What does the author argue is the key problem for democratic activists in Eastern Europe?
2. What prevented the rise of a new "left-wing" in Eastern Europe?
3. What is the public's main attitude toward civil society institutions in the region?

An early decision by civil society groups in the East to be apolitical has left them holding the bag for governments that shirk basic responsibilities.

Agnieszka Graff, "Activists: Treading Water," *Transitions Online* (www.tol.org), January 20, 2009, p. 1.

"We wanted a vibrant civil society, and all we got were NGOs [nongovernmental organizations]." I have heard this quote several times, sometimes attributed to an anonymous social activist in Hungary and other times to someone in the Czech Republic. Yet whoever said it first, it captures an important feeling haunting the region, which I would describe as disillusionment mixed with nostalgia and bitterness. For some 13 years (since returning from my studies abroad), I have been part of a circle of people in Poland who could be defined as "social activists," "engaged intelligentsia," or "the new Left"—feminists, human rights activists, and academics with an interest in social justice and political change, many of us linked to the former democratic opposition. Most [of us] would agree that something has gone wrong.

"We wanted a vibrant civil society, and all we got were NGOs [nongovernmental organizations]."

There seems to be a great distance between the time of wild hope and engagement in 1989 and the years that followed, and the present atmosphere of distrust, cynical me-ism, the low level of social activism, and the plague of burnout among activists. In my view, the sense of defeat and discouragement is connected with the way in which civil society was conceived and idealized in the late 1980s and early 1990s (i.e., as separate from the realm of politics), the way it congealed into institutions and was professionalized by the late 1990s (a process sometimes referred to as NGO-ization), and the way these institutions are now positioned in relationship to one another, the society, and the state.

Other forces and processes are also at play. . . . Such topics as education or the role of the Church are worth discussing, but I believe that the key problem is the relation of civil society to market forces, and the dominance of the neoliberal framework in the region's transition to democracy. It is to this that I devote the bulk of my response.

Rejecting Politics as Usual

I will not be the first to suggest that much of the sickness afflicting civil society in Eastern and central Europe is due to its conception from the very beginning as a sort of nonpolitical engagement, a mission that is not about power struggle, ideological difference, or group interests, but about serving the common good. The sources of this ethos, as we know, have their roots in the culture of political dissidence that arose in the 1970s and 1980s. The concept of "anti-politics" then survived 1989 largely unexamined and was idealized—both by activists and by institutions such as the UN [United Nations] and the EU [European Union]—as the proper site of the transition to democracy. I would argue, though, that in a democracy there is no such thing as political neutrality. There is no such thing as a commonly agreed definition of the common good. In effect, "anti-politics" has a politics of its own, in that it legitimizes the status quo. As an ideological construct, the glorification of "anti-politics" has served to constrain rather than encourage effective and autonomous organization, blocked debate about alternative paths of development, and, finally, contributed to the rise of right-wing populism.

In her recent book *Citizenship in an Enlarging Europe*, Barbara Einhorn describes what she calls the civil society trap: Instead of building a movement for social change, groups are engaged in "stopping the 'gap' left by state retrenchment and the ensuing loss of public welfare provisions." In this scenario, social actors such as women's rights activists are reduced to the role of mere service providers (and often inefficient ones, at that), a fig leaf in the process of mass privatization. The question is: Was this what we wanted? Is this what we meant by empowerment and democratization?

I consider the civil society trap to be part of a broader historical and social process, which is clear to me only in retrospect (things seemed natural and inevitable at the time). Early on in the transition period, the limited definition of "the political" led to a peculiar division of roles in the public sphere. State institutions and party politics, as well as the sphere of public debate, were soon conceived of as dirty and left to self-proclaimed experts, most of whom were uncritically committed to a neoliberal agenda and who viewed the process of marketization as nonnegotiable. Meanwhile, the "idealists" committed themselves to the purportedly neutral ideal of civil society.

In a democracy there is no such thing as political neutrality.

Idealism and Reality

Today, I think that these idealists, on the run from ideological commitment, were the very people who, in another scenario, might have offered a political alternative to the neoliberal paradigm. One that would have involved a social safety net that could and should have been provided by the state. Without the constricting ideal of "anti-politics," they might have transformed the public sphere, engaging people in a truly democratic debate about the possible paths of transition itself; they might have built a continuity of values with the political idealists of the pre-war period (stemming from the homegrown Socialist and not the post-Communist tradition). In short, had it not been for the "politics of anti-politics," a new left wing might have emerged, marginalizing the corrupt post-Communist forces and possibly preventing the rise of right-wing populism. Instead, with only a few exceptions (notably Jacek Kuron), efforts were chiefly poured into "serving society."

Meanwhile, as Kinga Dunin, Slawomir Sierakowski and others have argued, power in the public sphere was neatly divided between the market and the Church, the experts and the priests. Proclaiming themselves to be outsiders to both power and ideology, civil society actors were in no position to challenge this right-wing hegemony (neoliberal in economics and conservative in values). The key issues were never debated, because the answers had already been provided. No wonder the terms "democracy" and "civil society" came to ring hollow to so many people.

How did we end up in the blind alley of anti-politics? Chiefly because we left the politics to (mostly male) "experts." The idea that the free market should be allowed to rule with as little state regulation and intervention as possible was all but a dogma in the transition era. All those who challenged the neoliberal paradigm (or even called it a paradigm, suggesting that it could be up for debate), were labeled as ignoramuses, populists or nutcases. Jacek Kuron was seen as a saint—idealistic, but somewhat unrealistic and naive. The power of this ideology and the fear of stigma was (and perhaps still is) tremendous. Hence, instead of creating another political scenario, people who believed in social justice retreated into "anti-politics" instead of challenging neoliberal dogma; we engaged in damage limitation.

Power in the public sphere was neatly divided between the market and the Church, the experts and the priests.

The Role of NGOs

While it is true that NGOs helped a great deal at the local level, it could also be argued that they were supplying the

The Pessimism of Today Contrasts with the Optimism of the Past

Choosing the path of democracy, free markets, and freedom required great vision, courage, and moral leadership. Ten years ago, it was not the obvious choice, nor was it the easiest. But today in so many of your countries, there is no question that the path of free markets and democracy is the right choice. I have been privileged to visit many of your countries, and I have seen firsthand the struggle and the possibilities of reform. I have met many of the people and the organizations represented in this room and have seen with my own eyes how you have contributed to the transformation that is occurring. Certainly, I have seen that here in Poland. This nation is a testament to the fact that democratic and free market reforms, when decisively and thoroughly implemented, do work. It's been three years since I last came to Warsaw, and in those years, much has changed. New businesses and shopping centers are moving into neighborhoods. New cars are crowding once empty streets. Cell phones are ringing in cafes, parks, and sidewalks—that's an annoying indication of progress. But all of them are signs that a new middle class, the backbone of any democracy, is emerging.

Hillary Rodham Clinton, "Partners in Transition: Lessons for the Next Decade," Speech, Warsaw, Poland, October 5, 1999. http://clinton4.nara.gov.

neoliberal state with an alibi. For example, gender injustice leads to the formation of women's groups and NGOs, which provide services for women usually along single-issue lines (hotlines, legal advice, medical information, shelter for victims of violence, and sex education in schools). Occasionally, we also demonstrate, protest, or lobby, but service takes up most of our energy and resources. When protests do take place, state authorities are visibly uninterested: Why should the government be worried about gender discrimination when that is what women's NGOs are for? Feminism is thus reduced from a world-changing vision and grassroots political movement to a series of professionally run institutions engaging in projects, which are forced to adapt to outside agendas and pressures because of their dependence on funding.

If civil society is by definition marginal to state institutions, those state institutions are happy to take advantage of the fact, relegating activists to the status of service providers, or worse—charities. Twenty years down the road, many of the "idealists" I know are tired of this, and the politics of anti-politics is increasingly viewed as a dead end. It was as a consequence of this realization that initiatives such as the Greens 2004 [a political party], *Krytyka Polityczna* (Political Critique), and the Women's Party were created in Poland. All three are overtly political and define the public sphere as the site of the struggle for power. On the other hand, they are also idealistic in their commitment to social justice. I see this as a long overdue departure from the civil society model and an effort to reconnect politics and idealism.

Symptoms of a Disease

As the above diagnosis suggests, I see the disease ailing civil society as essentially systemic. It is therefore difficult to pinpoint specific problems that could be solved within the existing framework. Most of the difficulties I can see take me back to the original problem with "anti-politics," i.e., the civil society trap. Here are three examples.

First comes the massive public distrust of civil society institutions. This problem is one of alienation: For instance, many women complain about sexism, gender inequality, etc., but nonetheless do not view the women's movement as representing them, nor is there a grassroots organization they might join. On the contrary, the movement is perceived as a body of distant institutions, funded by a group of suspicious outsiders. "There's nowhere for us to go," I hear young feminists complain again and again. And indeed, the vast majority of NGOs are not membership organizations. Rather than a movement to join, there are foundations that can be applied to for financial support or appealed to (perhaps to protest against a sexist advertising campaign).

Some informal groups DO exist, and a politically minded young woman could surely find one to join. Yet the NGO model has become so much a part of the landscape that they, too, are perceived as service providers. Many activists complain about the cynical culture of disengagement and greed that surrounds us, and the fact that students consider it chic to be socially and politically apathetic. They are infuriated by the fact that people relate to us activists as clients, complaining and demanding, rather than contributing and becoming active themselves. Sadly, this is a result of the very framework we ourselves established—one of service, rather than representation. De-politicization and NGO-ization have had a profoundly alienating effect.

Secondly, there are bitter conflicts both within and among NGOs. I am not an expert on this painful subject, but I believe that it, too, is structural, and not to be solved by means of conflict resolution workshops, or the like. At its root is the very status and structure of NGOs, and above all the project-based funding system, which breeds ruthless competition for limited resources among people who theoretically have a common goal. The NGOs I know are also not managed democratically: In fact, the founder of any particular group often remains at the helm for decades. Even if the person in question is charismatic and deeply committed to the organization, its rigid power structure leads to conflicts and sometimes even its destruction.

Thirdly, I would mention the lack of success in transforming civil society initiatives into legislation. Many activists I know complain of the arrogance of politicians in communicating with NGOs. Despite the respectful talk of "dialogue with social partners," women's NGOs are often ignored when it comes to policy making. Without exonerating the politicians, who are indeed often arrogant, and need to be held accountable, I would argue that the problem is not just in political resistance to our demands (gender equality legislation, etc.). Rather, it is systemic: Once civil society had vacated the sphere of politics, social actors found themselves in a very weak negotiating position. Isolated NGOs (or even coalitions of NGOs) without large membership and grassroots support have very few means of exerting political pressure.

At its root is the very status and structure of NGOs, and above all the project-based funding system, which breeds ruthless competition for limited resources among people who theoretically have a common goal.

Breaking the Pattern

The problems listed above are interconnected, and all [are] related to the disadvantageous position of social activism with regard to the state and the market economy. I am convinced that by situating itself outside politics, civil society has contributed to its own marginalization. As I have argued above, the pattern is circular: The neoliberal state fails to deliver basic social provisions, and NGOs—funded mostly by Western institutions—respond to these needs by building professionalized, specialized structures designed to satisfy specific needs. The donors prefer nonpolitical projects (because of the assumptions of the civil society framework), and so depoliticization is strengthened further. As (some) needs are met, the state considers itself justified in its retrenchment strategy. Within civil society itself, there is less and less discussion of how to make the system more just and equitable, because organizations are busy writing grant applications for yet another project, which will help fill new gaps created by the unjust system.

I do not wish to negate the good that has come from the work of NGOs. There are many wonderful initiatives around, aimed to alleviate injustice, eradicate inequality, and fight prejudice. I continue to contribute to many, and have even helped to found some, including a feminist group and a stipend fund for young people who otherwise could not afford to study in Warsaw. I wish many others well. However, I believe that, in the final analysis, thinking of ourselves as remaining outside politics has been a costly mistake. Instead of getting to the roots of inequality and social exclusion, we ended up serving as a cushion to the very system we were protesting against.

It is not more NGOs to deal with more problems that are needed, but a shift in the framework itself: New voices in the public sphere and grassroots political movements that will encourage participation. We must begin to re-examine and move beyond the politics of anti-politics.

Viewpoint 4

Israel Struggles to Provide Equality for Minority Groups

David Newman

In this viewpoint, David Newman examines the problems faced by Arab-Israeli citizens. He contends that Israel has never adequately integrated its Arab citizens into the nation's broader political, economic, and social systems. One result is that Arab citizens have not enjoyed the full benefits of citizenship including economic development, and they face restrictions that Jewish citizens do not. Newman is a professor of politics and government at Ben-Gurion University of the Negev, and he is a frequent columnist for Israeli, American, and European newspapers.

As you read, consider the following questions:

1. According to the author, are Arab and Jewish settlements generally equally developed?
2. What is one of the main problems facing Arabs in Israel?
3. Does Israel officially grant equal rights to all citizens, according to the viewpoint?

Last week's comments [September 2009] by Minority Affairs Minister Avishay Braverman that the State of Israel should ask forgiveness from its Arab citizens for the way they

David Newman, "Borderline View: Israel's Democracy and Its Arab Population," *The Jerusalem Post*, October 5, 2009.

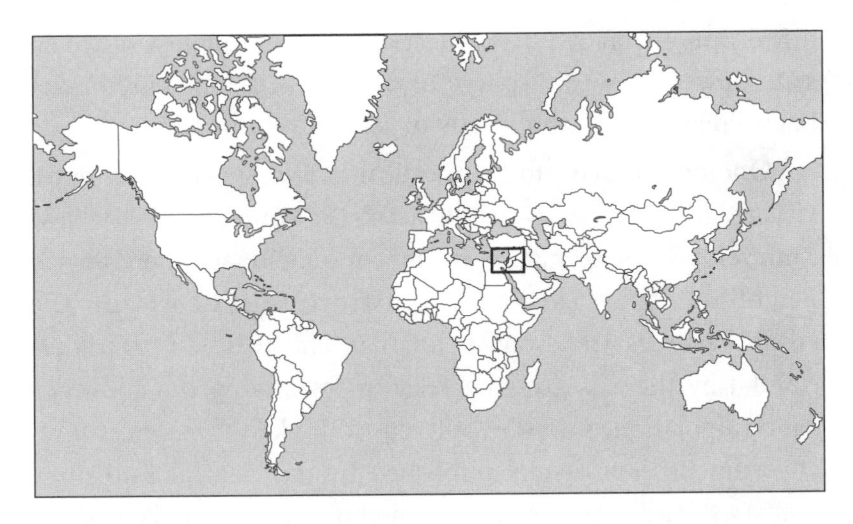

have been treated during 60 years of statehood, raised, yet again, one of the basic dilemmas facing Israel as a sovereign state—namely how to be a Jewish *and* democratic state.

It's not easy being a democracy, and it's even more difficult being a democracy when your country is self-defined as an exclusive nation-state. On top of that, it is almost impossible to be a democracy when the country's minority population (the Arab-Palestinian citizens of Israel) is part of a wider regional conflict in which it identifies (as would be expected) with the political and national aspirations of the neighbors, rather than of the state within which it resides.

Israel and Arab-Israelis

It is a dilemma Israel has faced since the day it was established, and it has never really been resolved. How, indeed, can a state define itself as being both Jewish (exclusive) and democratic (inclusive) at the same time? Democracy means a lot more than simply ensuring that everyone has the right to vote and be elected, regardless of ethnic or religious background. Democracy is about the ability of the state to fully integrate each of its citizens into every potential sphere of state activity. This includes equality in development, resource allocation, political appointments, even in achieving the highest office of state power—a whole sphere of activities that, it must be acknowledged, the Arab citizens of Israel do not enjoy.

One doesn't have to be a radical left-wing activist to pay a visit to any Arab town or village in the country and see how undeveloped these places are in comparison to their Jewish neighbors. The roads, the infrastructure systems and the school facilities are always below par, and it is easy to understand why there is growing resentment among the country's Arab population. And one only has to look at the annual local government data openly published by the Central Bureau of Statistics (and freely available on the government Web sites) to see that the Arab communities receive much fewer resources per capita than any of their Jewish counterparts, even the poor development towns.

Democracy is about the ability of the state to fully integrate each of its citizens into every potential sphere of state activity.

It is not easy to understand the rationale behind almost every government policy to allocate fewer resources per capita to Arab citizens. It doesn't make sense and, in the long term, has proved to be totally self-defeating for the state. The younger, more educated elements among the Arab population, who find it almost impossible to enter the job market at the same levels as their Jewish counterparts and who encounter silent discrimination in almost every sphere, have, as a result, become increasingly radicalized in their political opposition to the state on the one hand, and their support for the Palestinian cause on the other.

One of the biggest mistakes was the attempt by the state to create an artificial distinction between Arab citizens of Israel and Palestinians of the West Bank and Gaza. Prior to 1948, the Arab-Palestinian population residing between the Jordan River and the Mediterranean had been part of a single ethnic community, and this did not change as a result of the imposition of an artificial boundary drawn up in the Rhodes armistice talks.

Subsequently they have undergone separate processes of development, but they remain part and parcel of a single national entity. The sooner we accept their right to define their own identity, the greater the chance that we will be able to accept them for what they are—equal citizens with a minority identity—rather than always suspect them of constituting a fifth column.

One of the biggest mistakes was the attempt by the state to create an artificial distinction between Arab citizens of Israel and Palestinians of the West Bank and Gaza.

Arab-Israeli Land Development

The issue of land zoning for settlement expansion is but one of the more acute problems facing the Arab sector. It is ironic that the current Israeli government insists on the right of West Bank settlement expansion to enable internal natural growth of the existing settler population, while the same government does not enact the same principle for Arab citizens, who experience even more rapid internal growth. Their towns (euphemistically called "villages" in most statistical sources, even though they are much larger than equivalent Israeli development towns) are overcrowded and are prevented from growing by strict land-zoning laws. This is in stark contrast to the neighboring Jewish communities, which expand at much lower residential densities.

Given the context of the ongoing conflict between Arabs and Jews, Israel can justly be proud that it does accord equal political rights to all of its citizens, including those who iden-

Separate but Unequal

Despite the promise in Israel's Declaration of Independence of "complete equality of social and political rights," severe inequalities exist between Jewish and Arab Israelis. Arab citizens of Israel comprise 19.5% of the total population of the State of Israel numbering 1.37 million. Unlike the Palestinians in the territories, they are full citizens of Israel who vote and pay taxes, yet they suffer pervasive discrimination, unequal allocation of resources and violation of their legal rights. On an individual basis, Arab Israelis enjoy formal equality, including voting rights, freedom of worship and expression.

New Israel Fund, "Background: Arab Citizens of Israel," www.nif.org.

tify with the Palestinian cause. The fact that an Arab member of Knesset [legislature of Israel] can make a speech negating the very essence of the Jewish state within which he lives may not be comfortable for most ears, but it reflects a high level of freedom of speech that few other countries in similar situations would allow.

But that does not mean that we can expect the Arab-Palestinian citizens of the country to salute a flag, or sing an anthem, that has been designed to characterize and represent the Jewish and Zionist symbols of statehood. We need to be much more realistic in what to expect from the Arab population while demonstrating to them that we believe they can be fully integrated—politically, socially and economically—within every facet of life. If we succeeded in doing that, we would become a much better democracy than we like to think we are already.

This does not mean having to reduce, in any way, the Jewish characteristics and symbols of statehood, the *raison d'etre* of why the State of Israel was established in the first place. But it does mean recognizing that democracies are judged by their policies toward their minorities and those groups that do not have power, far more than by the simple technicality of whether or not they are able to vote.

Viewpoint 5

North Korea Ignores Human Rights and Democracy

Kay Seok

In the following viewpoint, Kay Seok contends that the current North Korean regime ignores the basic wants and needs of its population. Even as the government has allowed some reforms designed to introduce limited free market principles following a famine in the 1990s, it continues to repress human rights and democracy. Nonetheless, an increasing number of North Koreans are ignoring restrictions in order to gain a better life. Seok is a researcher who specializes in North Korean politics and society for the group Human Rights Watch.

As you read, consider the following questions:

1. According to Seok, how many people died in North Korea during the famine of the 1990s?
2. Which democratic country is the world's thirteenth largest economy?
3. How many people does the Kaesong Industrial Complex in North Korea employ, according to the viewpoint?

The true Communists starved to death at home, silent, obediently waiting for the state to come and save them. At least, that's what some North Koreans say, only half in jest.

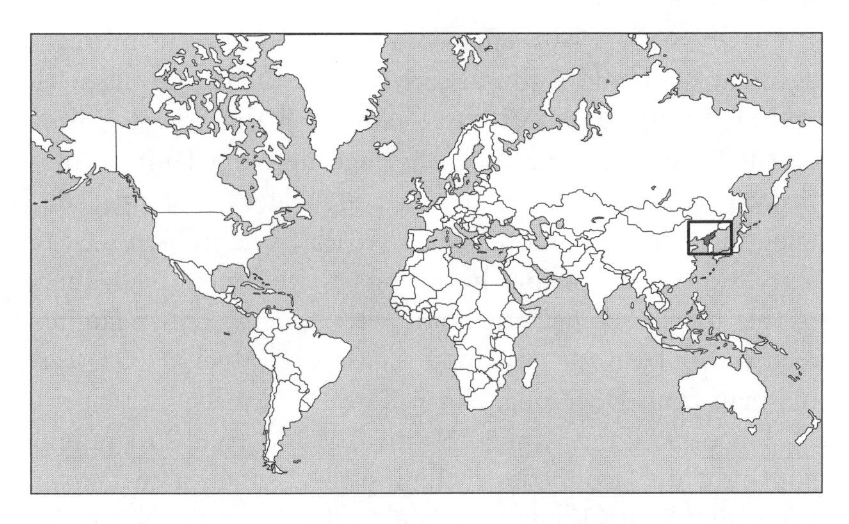

Few expect a humanitarian disaster—a famine, say—to bring anything good to any society. But in North Korea, the famine in the mid-1990s that killed a million people also led to positive change. In the very struggle people waged to survive the famine, the state lost much of its control over their daily lives. North Koreans became more self-reliant and inventive; they found ways to survive, and also to make money, replacing the almost defunct ration system with a growing market economy.

Famine and Aid

Before the famine, North Korea was a country befitting the title "Hermit Kingdom." The 20 million people had no source of information but state media, which print and broadcast only Workers' Party propaganda. Traveling outside one's immediate area of residency was banned, except for family weddings and funerals. The state intelligence agency ran a tight monitoring operation against its own people, tasking one out of every five households with informing on others. Most importantly, the state dominated food distribution, which kept everyone subservient and immobile for fear of losing their only access to sustenance.

By the early 1990s, after decades of government mismanagement of the agricultural sector, years of natural disasters, and an abrupt end to barter trade with the Soviet Union, North Korea's chronic food shortage developed into a full-fledged famine. By the mid-1990s, the state had stopped distributing rations to most people. At least one million died of starvation, waiting for the rations to resume. "Back then, people died of hunger, at home, very quietly. Entire families died without anyone noticing for days, even weeks," a 38-year-old man from Hoeryong, North Korea, told me.

Since 1995, the [United Nations] World Food Programme and individual countries including the United States, Japan, China and South Korea have sent food aid, but the North Korean government continued to impose severe restrictions on the monitoring of aid distribution by limiting the areas aid workers could visit, how often they could, and requiring at least a week of advance notice prior to such visits. Some humanitarian agencies accused the North Korean government of diverting aid to the military, instead of feeding the most vulnerable populations as intended. It's true, however, that even North Korean soldiers could not avoid hunger. A man in his early 30s from Hwanghae told me how half a dozen soldiers in his 100-strong unit died of hunger, while many others were sent home, because they were too malnourished to serve.

Before the famine, North Korea was a country befitting the title "Hermit Kingdom." The 20 million people had no source of information but state media.

Survival Strategies

But not everyone stayed put and starved. A massive number of North Koreans sold all their belongings, packed their bags and traveled from the cities to the countryside, where food was more readily available from collective farms and kitchen gardens. Needless to say, most of them didn't have permission to travel. But the authorities were unable to stop them, because even police officers were out hunting for food. The restriction of movement, with which North Korea controlled its population, began to break down. "I began spending my days not watching people but trying to find food for my family. The rations I received were not enough. We were desperate," a former intelligence official from North Korea described the hunger that even he, a member of the elite, could not escape.

Hundreds of thousands of North Koreans, mostly those who lived near the Chinese border, escaped to China to find food and work. Tens of thousands were arrested and repatriated to North Korea as "illegal migrants," while others voluntarily returned home to feed their families and use their newly acquired knowledge or skills to make money. These returnees brought back news from the outside world, undistorted by official propaganda. Echoing a new attitude of North Koreans who survived through the famine, a 19-year-old woman from Hoeryong, North Korea, said, "The last time my family received a state ration was early 1994. Since then, we have been on our own. If you depend on the state these days, you would starve to death."

Marketization

Meanwhile, markets sprang up all over North Korea, replacing the now almost defunct ration system as the main source of food. At first, the markets operated on the barter system, where desperately hungry people could exchange anything valuable for food, but they gradually developed into places where people bought and sold anything and everything to make a profit. Now in the capital, Pyongyang, and beyond, the country is teeming with bustling markets where people buy and sell necessities, using the North Korean won, Chinese yuan and even U.S. dollars. A 40-year-old man from Hyesan, North Korea, explained that merchants these days prefer U.S. dollars or Chinese yuan. "They don't trust the North Korean won. I even heard rumors that the richer merchants have piles of dollars hidden at home," he said.

Nowadays, North Korean citizens are engaged in all kinds of businesses, ranging from selling homemade noodles to running express buses to real estate development. Private land transactions are illegal, and therefore unprotected, yet across the country, residential real estate is bought and sold, from urban apartments to farmhouses. Usually, a buyer and a seller will exchange cash, then go to the local housing authority and bribe the official to change the tenant's name, rubber-stamping the illicit purchase and giving the buyer rights to the home. An 18-year-old girl from Kaechon, North Korea, described the private bus operations in her city. "You go to the bus terminal, and you choose between state-run and privately owned buses, based on the condition of the buses and the departure schedule. The government knows, of course. They collect fees from people who run bus operations."

Echoing words of many other North Koreans, a 60-year-old woman from Wonsan told me, "In North Korea, people now only care about making money."

On the darker side, the same motivation to make profit is also boosting socially destructive businesses such as the trade in illicit drugs.

Money Talks

However, without people intending or even realizing the implications, some activities motivated by profit have led to more access to information: the roaring trade in imported CDs and DVDs of South Korean soap operas and movies, for instance. Since many North Koreans still don't have enough to eat, it may seem odd that people would spend money on entertainment, but the fact is that North Koreans are hungry not only for food but also for diversion. "I would trade a meal for a South Korean movie," said one North Korean teenager. "Food is not all you need to survive."

After years of the infiltration of South Korean pop culture into North Korea now it appears to be common knowledge for North Korea's urban residents that South Korea is far richer and freer than they are—South Korea now ranks as the world's 13th largest economy and a democracy, while North Korea remains a poor dictatorship. Until about a decade ago, however, most North Koreans "knew" South Korea as a desperately poor country, its capital, Seoul, filled with prostitutes and beggars. They also "understood" that North Korea was a "workers' paradise" going through temporary difficulties because of US sanctions.

On the darker side, the same motivation to make profit is also boosting socially destructive businesses such as the trade in illicit drugs. A truck driver in his early 30s told me he was taking *bingdu*, also called *uhrum*, (meaning "ice," referring to methamphetamine) to stay awake for long hours of driving. A high school girl told me she bought a cold medicine at a market from a merchant, but later found out it was bingdu, and another said many of her classmates tried it out of curiosity. One young man in his 20s said he took it with friends recreationally. They all shrugged off concerns about its addictive nature.

Government's Response

Of course, not all has changed in North Korea. Kim Jong-il's government still holds unchallenged power, and continues to run a prison-camp system that enslaves tens of thousands of people, including young children. And it periodically executes people publicly, for offences such as stealing state property or other "anti-Communist" behavior. North Koreans also complain of the ever-rising level of corruption and extortion by officials. A woman in her 40s from Hoeryong, North Korea, described how about a third of her income from markets was

North Korea's Repression

All institutions are controlled by the state or by the ruling party. There are no independent broadcast media, newspapers, political parties, civic associations, trade unions, or any other type of organization essential to the development of civil society in a modern society.

There is no freedom of religion; indeed, the government permits religious worship only by organizations approved by and linked to the state. The ownership of a Bible (sometimes distributed by Christian groups on the border with China) is illegal and can result in imprisonment or even execution. The state controls all aspects of the economy, including the production and sale of grain and other goods. Freedom of movement is restricted. As in Cuba, it is treasonous to try to leave the country, although tens of thousands have attempted to cross to South Korea. In contravention of international human rights conventions that protect the rights of refugees, the Chinese government has returned refugees to North Korea, where they are often imprisoned or executed.

Democracy Web, "Comparative Studies in Freedom," www.democracyweb.org.

taken by various officials. "The housing official, the electricity official, the water official . . . as soon as they smell your money, they are on you," she told me. "They will find some excuse, some violation you have committed. You have to pay up. There is no avoiding them."

Meanwhile, state enterprises, run by the Workers' Party, the military or sometimes the parliament, dominate the most profitable businesses, such as natural resources, seafood and mushrooms, mostly for export. The government also has been trying hard to regain some of the control it lost during the famine, often in vain. For example, between late 2005 and early 2006, it tried to ban the buying and selling of rice, North Korea's staple, at the markets. But because the state was not able to offer an alternative, merchants continued to sell rice secretly. The policy failed.

In 2007, the government banned women below a certain age (the specific age varied from 30, 40 or even 49 years, depending on time, location and sources) from doing business at markets to force them to return to their state-designated jobs. According to recent reports, the ban largely failed, because state jobs pay very little, if at all. An 18-year-old woman from Pyongsong told me how her older sister earned 1,500 to 2,000 North Korean won ($US10 to $13 at the official exchange rate, but only equivalent to $0.40 to $0.60 on the black market) per month as a nurse. After contribution to the Workers' Party and other mandatory donations, her monthly income bought only about a kilogram of rice. Simply put, most North Koreans have no choice but to find a non-state source of income.

Since late 2004, North Korea also threatened harsher punishment for those leaving the country without state permission. The government announced repeatedly that the "violators" would be sent to prison for several years, instead of several months as before. This new policy has certainly helped boost the bribes that border guards pocket from "illegal" border crossers, and the number of border crossers dropped significantly in the past couple of years, but it still has not stopped them completely. Merchants with financial resources still go to China by bribing border guards, while human traffickers continue to bring desperately poor North Korean women and girls as young as 16 to Chinese farmers as brides.

At the same time, the North Korean authorities are also trying to take advantage of the societal changes that took place. Private citizens who do business at markets instead of reporting to their state-designated jobs must actually pay a "contribution" to their workplaces, often amounting to many times the value of their state salary, in order to avoid prison sentences. A 24-year-old man from Hungnam, North Korea, explained how it works. "You skip work, which pays you nothing, and go make money at a market. But if you just skip work, they will come and get you. So, you pay up. Then they will leave you alone."

Last but not least, the North Korean government started a couple of major cash-generating projects in collaboration with South Korean businesses, after relations between the two countries warmed thanks to a policy of engagement by former South Korean presidents Kim Dae-jung and Roh Mu-hyun. The North Korean government has opened the scenic Geumgangsan, or Diamond Mountain, and more recently the city of Kaesong, to South Korean tourists. In June 2004, it opened the Kaesong Industrial Complex, which now employs 23,000 North Korean workers who manufacture a range of products including watches, shoes, clothes, kitchenware, and car parts for mostly South Korean businesses. Such projects continue to remain a precious source of cash for the North Korean government, regardless of politics between the two countries.

North Korea has long lacked high-quality seed, chemical fertilizer and fuel for machinery, and largely remains unfamiliar with advanced agricultural technologies.

Hunger Persists

North Korea recovered from the famine, but food shortages persist. North Korea has long lacked high-quality seeds, chemical fertilizer and fuel for machinery, and largely remains unfamiliar with advanced agricultural technologies. The environmental degradation of hills and mountains caused by people cutting down trees for use as fuel leads to floods in the summer, damaging crops. As a result, North Korea has no option but to depend upon international aid to make up for the shortage. Amid reports of rising prices of rice, corn and other staples in North Korea, *choongoong*, or spring food shortage, already arrived. As of this writing [April 14, 2008], the North Korean government has yet to request food aid from the new, conservative South Korean government of Lee Myung-bak, who vowed to properly monitor aid distribution, unlike his two predecessors. For North Koreans, it appears to be yet another hungry year.

For many North Koreans, the changes—both positive and negative—set in motion by the famine are irreversible. In fact, many North Koreans I met, especially the young, said they want more change. Their specific wishes ranged from the frivolously mundane, such as wearing whatever clothes they liked, to the seriously political, such as a desire for North Korea's reforms and openness. They are survivors of the worst humanitarian disaster the country has seen in half a century. Compared to their parents, they are far more informed, open-minded, and brave. And they will continue to push for more changes.

Periodical Bibliography

The following articles have been selected to supplement the diverse views presented in this chapter.

Jelke Boesten	"Revisiting 'Democracy in the Country and at Home' in Peru," *Democratization*, April 2010.
Sean Brooks	"Legitimising Khartoum," AlJazeera.net, April 2010. http://english.aljazeera.net.
Akua Djanie	"What Are We Really Celebrating?" *New African*, February 1, 2010.
Tamara Eidelman	"Arrival of Russian Democracy: March 26, 1989," *Russian Life*, March–April 2009.
Takis Fotopoulos	"Liberal and Socialist 'Democracies' Versus Inclusive Democracy," *International Journal of Inclusive Democracy*, January 2006.
Linda Frum	"The Real Trouble at Rights and Democracy," *Maclean's*, March 22, 2010.
Isabel Hilton	"This Restless Land," *New Statesman*, October 15, 2009.
Maclean's	"How to Fix Democracy: Step One . . . ," October 6, 2009.
Fernando Molina	"The Historical Dynamics of Ethnic Conflicts: Confrontational Nationalisms, Democracy and the Basques in Contemporary Spain," *Nations & Nationalism*, March 11, 2010.
Yin Pumin	"Granting Equality," *Beijing Review*, March 23, 2010.
Carina Ray	"The Empire's Ghost Returns," *New African*, August 1, 2009.
USA Today Magazine	"Gender Inequality in a Land of Democracy," April 2008.

CHAPTER 3

Democracy and Economics

Viewpoint 1

Sri Lanka Faces Economic Implications While Demilitarizing and Expanding Democracy

Darini Rajasingham Senanayake

In the following viewpoint, Darini Rajasingham Senanayake, an anthropologist and visiting fellow at the Institute of Southeast Asian Studies in Singapore, notes that Sri Lanka was once regarded as a strong democracy. However, during the past thirty years, the government has been engaged in a civil war with ethnic Tamil rebels. The end of the conflict did not stop militarization within the country, according to the author. Instead the government has continued to expand its military and security services at the expense of efforts to restore democracy and human rights in the strife-torn country.

As you read, consider the following questions:

1. What is the name of the main antigovernment, rebel group in Sri Lanka?
2. By how many more soldiers does the government intend to increase its military in the aftermath of the civil war?
3. Which side, the government or the LTTE, broke the 2008 ceasefire, according to the viewpoint?

Darini Rajasingham Senanayake, "De-militarising Democracy and Governance in Sri Lanka," Aliran, October 3, 2009. Reproduced by permission.

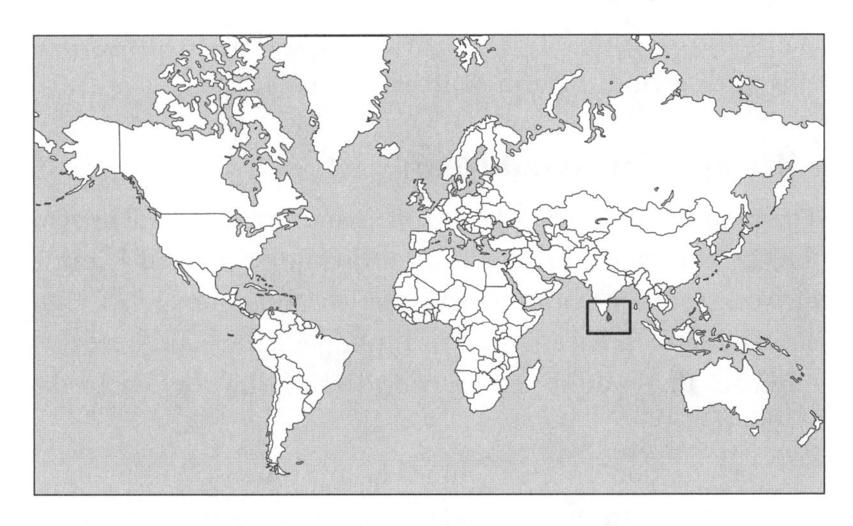

Sri Lanka was once a 'model democracy' with a welfare state and social indicators that were the envy of the developing world. Hence, there was great optimism that life would return to normal, the barriers and checkpoints come down, tourists and foreign investments flow back, and the economy finally takes off in an environment of peace and security once the Liberation Tigers of Tamil Eelam (LTTE) were defeated. Residents of central Colombo [the largest city in Sri Lanka] who are daily inconvenienced by the security arrangements of the President and various VIPs that had turned the city into a veritable battlefield had hoped to see the barriers and checkpoints go. They have been disappointed!

After the defeat of the LTTE [in May 2009], it was hoped that South Asia's most desirable capital city, whose many beautiful trees had been cut down to enhance VIP security, would once again become people, pedestrian and environment-friendly now that the war was over. Residents of Colombo also looked forward to an end to the culture of politicians breaking speed limits with impunity and the lifting of Emergency Regulations (ER), which had also been used and abused by the State during the southern Janatha Vimukthi Peramuna

(JVP) uprising in the late eighties and early nineties when tens of thousands died in southern Sri Lanka.

After the War, What Next?

These hopes have been dashed. It is increasingly evident that the Colombo regime's insecurities (despite or perhaps because of weeks of vainglorious victory celebrations), coupled with 30 years of war, have left an institutional legacy and 'security' mind-set that would need a considerable shift before Lanka takes off.

The question on many minds at this time is: Will militarisation be a substitute for democratisation—beyond the show of elections? The impact of 30 years of armed conflict between successive Sri Lankan governments and the Liberation Tigers of Tamil Eelam (LTTE), may be analysed in terms of human, economic, and governance costs.

It is increasingly clear that the governance cost and democracy deficit would have the greatest long-term impact on the country. The human costs of three decades of conflict are evident in over 100,000 lives lost and maimed and over half a million displaced at different times including the 280,000 in internment camps in Vavuniya at this time. The mounting economic cost of conflict is evident in the fact that in the final year of war the government was spending almost 17 per cent of GDP [gross domestic product] on the war effort. This is partly the reason for a 1.9 billion IMF [International Monetary Fund] loan request at this time. Sri Lanka has the largest armed forces per capita in South Asia and has trouble paying salaries. Yet, strangely since the war ended there are plans to enlarge the military by 50 per cent—an odd sort of military Keynesianism [theory based on the ideas of twentieth-century economist John Maynard Keynes] given that the country does not produce its own arms and spends billions on armaments that it can hardly afford.

Much work lies ahead if the narrative of economic boom in Lanka is to be realised. The challenge now is to move beyond a highly militarised, state-centric national security paradigm and prioritise human security and development, which enabled the island to achieve the highest social indicators in South Asia. It is thus that the military victory over the LTTE may be translated into a stable and sustainable peace in Sri Lanka.

The human costs of three decades of conflict are evident in over 100,000 lives lost and maimed and over half a million displaced at different times including the 280,000 in internment camps in Vavuniya.

Governance Cost of Conflict and Militarisation

The last three years of war to defeat the LTTE saw a serious erosion of governance structures, democratic institutions, and traditions of multiculturalism and co-existence among diverse ethnic and religious communities. It is clear that post-LTTE, the government would need to rethink the military-centric national security state and the repression that it cultivated during the war, which in some ways mimicked the tactics and strategies of the enemy which ran a quasi-state for a few years in the Vanni.

In his book *Brave New World Order*, Jack Nelson-Pallmeyer identified several characteristics of a National Security State, the primary one of which is "the military not only guarantees the security of the state against all internal and external enemies, it has enough power to determine the overall direction of the society. In a National Security State, the military exerts important influence over political, economic, as well as military affairs. . . . Authentic democracy depends on participation of the people. National Security States limit such participation in a number of ways: They sow fear and thereby narrow the range of public debate. They restrict and distort information; and they define policies in secret and implement those policies through covert channels and clandestine activities. The state justifies such actions through rhetorical pleas of 'higher purpose' and vague appeals to 'national security.'"

Thirty years of war had significant impact on democratic institutions in Sri Lanka. During the final push to defeat the LTTE, the government discredited the idea of peace. Those opposed to war and those who spoke for human rights were termed 'traitors'. Since the war ended, the government plans to build a war museum rather than a peace and reconciliation museum. An astrologer who predicted difficult days ahead for the powers-that-be in Colombo was recently arrested and would be under observation for three months.

The last three years of war to defeat the LTTE saw a serious erosion of governance structures, democratic institutions, and traditions of multiculturalism and coexistence among diverse ethnic and religious communities.

Meanwhile, according to the army commander, the military would be expanded by 50,000, even though the war is over and Sri Lanka has one of the largest militaries per capita in South Asia. The recruitment of additional troops to man camps in the northeast is of particular concern and suggests that rather than restore substantive democracy, the government plans a form of military occupation with the collusion of allied Tamil paramilitary groups. Moderate Tamil voices remain marginalised and have raised questions regarding the legitimacy of elections in a region with such a large displaced population.

While the country is broke and in need of an IMF loan to pay among other things the salaries of soldiers and an enormous cabinet of ministers, which includes a number of the President's relatives, the mind-set of militarism lives on. The

Sri Lankan government's internment of 280,000 Tamils, some of whom were witnesses to war crimes and may give evidence, in barbwire fenced camps and its treatment of them as a national security threat after claiming to have 'rescued' them from the LTTE; as well as, the failure to lift Emergency Rule and disarm paramilitaries in the north and east; the phenomenon of white van abductions of journalists, and the failure to start a process of demilitarisation and reconciliation with the minorities have led the United States to extend travel warnings for those wishing to visit Sri Lanka. It seems unlikely that Western tourists would return any time soon.

The Erosion of Rights

It is axiomatic that, as externalised threats are perceived and nations go to war, civil liberties and rights in the domestic sphere are eroded. This phenomenon was observed by Max Weber, a founding father of the discipline of sociology. While a number of ministries have proliferated those that actually have power to make and implement policy are few and controlled by the President and his brothers. Nepotism is extremis! During the last few years of the conflict, development projects were required to go through and get clearance from the Defence Ministry. Such centralisation has weakened democracy and strengthened the grip of the ruling family on power. One Rajapakse [referring to family members of Sri Lankan president Mahinda Rajapaksa] is Defence Secretary and the other, a nonelected member of parliament, who also controls reconstruction in the north and east. It is widely understood that together the triumvirate control 70 per cent of the economy via control of key ministries.

Within days of the celebrations following the capture of LTTE's de facto capital in January 2009, one of the island's leading journalists, Lasantha Wickrematunge, editor in chief of the *Sunday Leader* newspaper, a liberal antiestablishment paper known for exposing corruption and nepotism in the

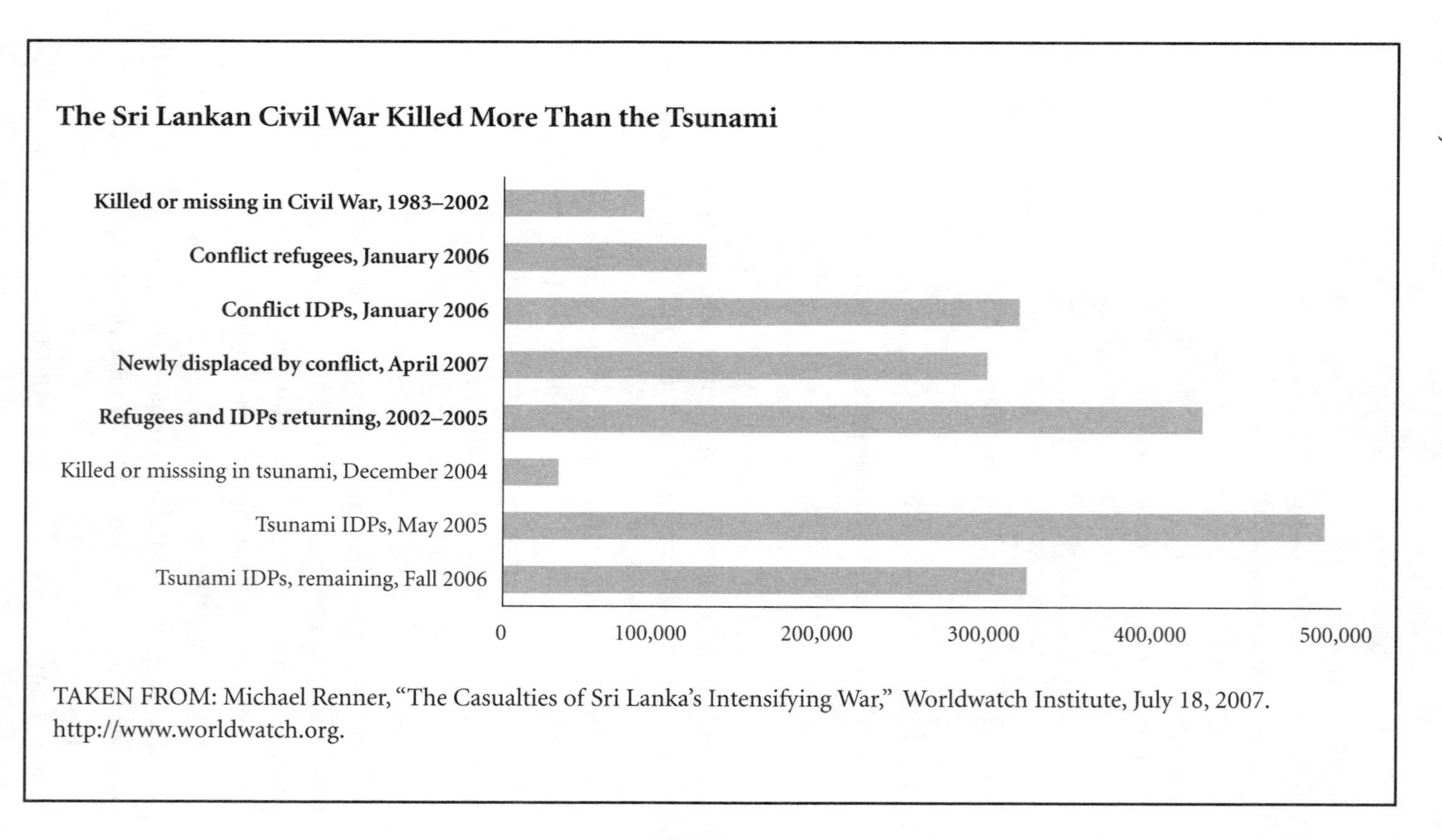

The Sri Lankan Civil War Killed More Than the Tsunami

TAKEN FROM: Michael Renner, "The Casualties of Sri Lanka's Intensifying War," Worldwatch Institute, July 18, 2007. http://www.worldwatch.org.

state apparatus, was assassinated in broad daylight in Colombo. At his funeral, where thousands gathered, an effigy of Sri Lanka's President, Mahinda Rajapaksa, was burnt. The slain journalist's funeral was attended by political leaders, media representatives, civil society organisations and senior foreign diplomats in Colombo. The slain journalist, who was also a lawyer, had penned his own obituary three days before his assassination: "And then they came for me", naming in all but words his killers. His final editorial published posthumously which has come to be known as the 'letter from the grave' constitutes a powerful indictment on the regime that would be hard to shake off in a country where astrology, the symbolic and uncanny, carries significant weight in politics. Minimally, the state remains accused of promoting a 'culture of impunity', which has rendered Sri Lanka 'one of the world's most dangerous places for journalists', according to Reporters Without Borders. In the past two years, at least eight journalists have been killed in the country, according to the Committee to Protect Journalists.

As the war (including an information war) escalated, the phenomenon of extrajudicial killings rose. Wickramatunge's assassination was in the wake of a series of killings and intimidation of journalists and lawyers, and attacks on independent media institutions in the south. In August 2008, Sri Lanka lost its seat in the United Nations Human Rights Council and has since turned down several requests by the United Nations [Commission on] Human Rights to set up an observer mission to monitor the situation in the country. At the end of the war, the United Nations [Commission on] Human Rights called for an independent inquiry into war crimes by the parties to the conflict.

The culture of militarisation and impunity that the conflict had enabled needs to be rolled back. Sri Lanka has one of the largest standing armies per capita in South Asia and alternative jobs would be necessary for the over 200,000 troops.

The military victory over the LTTE is only one-half of the solution to building a peaceful and stable polity. It would also be necessary to address the intragroup dynamics of conflict. Many of those who fought and died and were disabled were from poor rural communities and marginalised caste groups. A war economy had grown, and many of the rural poor worked as soldiers and (women go as housemaids to the Middle East). In a time of rising unemployment due to the global recession, it would be necessary to boost the economy and provide jobs.

In the past two years, at least eight journalists have been killed in the country.

Terrorism and Democracy in Sri Lanka

The 'invincibility' of the Liberation Tigers of Tamil Eelam and the terror threat they posed to world peace may have been often exaggerated. There were several reasons for the defeat of the LTTE. Principal among them was the changing global security environment that became increasingly hostile to groups that used terrorist methods post-9/11 [after the September 11, 2001, terrorist attacks on the United States], as well as the egotism and compounding mistakes of the LTTE leader [Velupillai] Prabhakaran, principal among which was the assassination of Rajiv Gandhi, the former Prime Minister of India. Prior to 9/11 and the global war on terror, the LTTE and its transnational network had grown and benefited from a period of relatively unfettered globalisation at the end of the Cold War, also given considerable international sympathy for the plight of the minority Tamil-speaking peoples in Sri Lanka. It was recognised that one man's terrorist may be another's liberation fighter.

After 9/11, with the global 'war on terror' there was far less international space and tolerance for the organisation to manoeuvre. The government capitalised on this fact by renaming the conflict in Sri Lanka a 'war on terror', soliciting international assistance to shut down the LTTE's funding and supply networks from the diaspora. While the Rajapakse government waged a determined battle against the organisation after abrogating the Norwegian-brokered cease-fire in 2008, and provided the armed forces all that was needed by way of arms, ammunition, and men, the international context that had made the LTTE apparently invincible in the previous decades had changed. It is also arguable that the demise of the LTTE was also largely due to its leader's egotism and the compounding of mistakes, including the assassination of Rajiv Gandhi, which had turned India against the group.

The government of Sri Lanka has very successfully assembled a group of Asian donors, prominent among them China, Japan and India to counterbalance Western criticism of its conduct of the last days of the conflict. These donors place less value on human security and human rights and tend to have a state-centric approach to security. The need to move beyond state-centric security discourses and address the root causes of conflicts in South Asia from a post-war-on-terror paradigm is, however, increasingly apparent.

The Dangers of Militarisation

Since 9/11, instead of measured and targeted responses to terrorist acts, militarisation and advocacy for military solutions have sometimes exacerbated and aggravated the root causes of conflicts that require social and political-economic solutions. Social sector and welfare state spending has been reduced with the claim that development cannot occur without defence, even though the poverty and conflict trap is a consequence of the transfer of resources that accompanies ballooning defence expenditure, socioeconomic decline, increased regional and economic inequality, structural violence and aid dependence. Increasingly, it is obvious that inclusive development and peace building is necessary for regional security in Sri Lanka, and you can't have one without the others.

In the last three years, militarisation and the 'national security state' had become pervasive with a significant erosion of Sri Lanka's democratic traditions and institutions. While the military victory over the LTTE is conclusive and there is little chance that it would regroup and return any time soon, the military victory needs to be converted into a stable and sustainable peace. Other long-term, low-intensity, ethnonational conflicts in the region point to the fact that groups fighting for autonomy or rights for minorities may regroup and return years or decades later as was the case in Nepal and Aceh, Indonesia, unless there is a political solution that addresses the root causes of conflict. To ensure a sustainable peace the government would need to win the confidence of minority cultural groups, work toward reconciliation and address the root causes of the conflict. Simultaneously, it would be necessary to repair a dysfunctional democracy whose institutions were significantly eroded in the course of decades of war-induced emergency rule, which the government has still not lifted.

Viewpoint 2

India's Political Struggles Undermine Its Middle Class

P.V. Indiresan

According to P.V. Indiresan in the following viewpoint, India's main political parties are not addressing the needs and desires of the nation's growing middle class. Instead, the author contends, the rich are accumulating an increasing share of the country's wealth, while core services for the middle class are not being delivered and programs to help raise the poor out of poverty are not being implemented. Indiresan is a scholar, an author, and a former director of the Indian Institute of Science, Madras.

As you read, consider the following questions:

1. According to the viewpoint, what are the common worries or concerns of the Indian middle class?
2. Who developed the Washington Consensus?
3. In the viewpoint, does the author argue that exports will increase or decrease for India in the near future?

> Under democracy one party always devotes its energies in trying to prove that the other party is unfit to rule—and both commonly succeed and are right.
>
> —*H.L. Mencken*

P.V. Indiresan, "Problem of Governance, Not Economics," *The Hindu Business Line*, April 26, 2009.

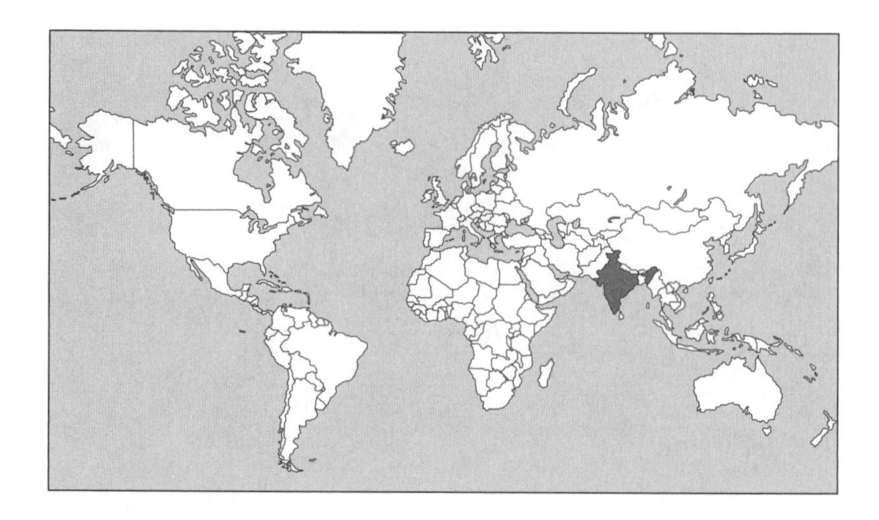

This is a saying that fits our political parties too, except that we have not two but any number of parties. India is a poor country with innumerable problems, many of them intractable. Common sense indicates that in a general election, political parties will discuss and debate at least some of those issues and suggest what they would do to resolve them. Unfortunately, India's elections are not moved by common sense. In the entire debate during the current elections, no party has a word to say on any of the problems that beset us.

Indifferent to Progress

The purpose of a general election is to win votes. Unfortunately, many of our voters are indifferent to progress. I recollect asking villagers in a poor area of Tamil Nadu what they wanted most. They were unanimous about a bridge over a *nullah* for a lane that led to their burial ground. The villagers were very poor; they used to get barely one full meal a day. They were all labourers who went to the tehsil headquarters every day selling their physical labour. Their needs must be many but all that they wanted was a bridge to their burial ground over a *nullah* which was unlikely to flood more than once or twice a year.

On the other hand, the middle class has several worries, typically, corruption, insecurity, criminalisation, unemployment, increasing disparity and inflation. All over the country, several middle-class groups have expressed their concerns on issues of this kind. They are overwhelmed by a feeling of helplessness because politicians of all hues are unanimously disinterested on such issues.

In these meetings, a number of issues are raised. Recently, a top journalist of the country gave out over 20 such issues but declined to suggest any solution with the retort: I am a journalist trained to ask questions but not to answer them!

Conceded we do need journalists who will raise questions, even unpleasant ones, we also need someone who will look for answers. Regrettably, there are few of them. Even if they suggest solutions, there is no one among business houses, politicians and bureaucracy to listen. Each one of them lives in a world of uncertainty and yet is not disposed to listen to advice—unless it is from an international 'expert'.

For instance, in the case of the economy, there is a general feeling that whatever may happen to the West, China and India will pull through. That optimism should be weighed against pessimistic business forecasts, loss of export markets and general decline in the economy. Will the Indian economy balance an increase in local consumption to match loss of exports? No one is certain.

The State Is Crucial

In the past 25 years, businesses have been moved by what is known as the Washington Consensus—a list of axioms proposed by John Williamson, an economist of the [Peterson] Institute for International Economics. His axioms were based on the view the market corrects itself and is best left alone to do so. Hence, the state should do all in its power to strengthen the markets and, for that reason, deregulate as far as possible.

Fifty years ago, Professor R.H. Tawney explained the opposite concept: It is not till it is discovered that high individual incomes will not purchase the mass of mankind immunity from cholera, typhus and ignorance, still less secure them the positive advantages of educational opportunity and economic security, that slowly and reluctantly, amid prophesies of moral degeneration and economic disaster, society begins to make collective provision for needs no ordinary individual, even if he works overtime all his life, can provide himself.

In other words, the state is crucial for any modern economy and that holds good for India too.

The Real Danger

The nuclear deal, the NREGA [National Rural Employment Guarantee Act] and Bharat Nirman [an infrastructure improvement program] are claimed by the Congress party as their greatest achievements, with the JNNURM [Jawaharlal Nehru National Urban Renewal Mission] as an honourable mention. Will expanding these achievements restore the growth rate of the country and generate enough employment for the increasing numbers of youth that are entering the labour market? Do the other parties have any better solution?

The fact remains that while the country has grown rapidly, disparities between the rich and the poor too [have] increased alarmingly.

According to reports, there are so few jobs for graduates that banks have been forced to offer special relief to outgoing students.

Hence, on college campuses (even among a few IIT [Indian Institute of Technology] graduates) worry about unemployment has begun to take root. Their numbers can become uncomfortably large soon, very soon. That is a real danger.

Increasing Women in India's Parliament

Today's Lok Sabha, or House of the People, as India's lower chamber is known, contains 58 women, a record number, but fewer than 11% of the seats. By greatly boosting women's membership of India's legislatures, the proposed amendment, its supporters say, will also begin to make a dent in their more grievous suffering—in a country where female fetuses are often aborted, where wives are battered and women earn on average $1,200 a year, less than a third of the male average. A woman can take credit for this: Sonia Gandhi, Congress's leader, who has pushed the long-mothballed bill against a furious band of dissenters—of a kind that persuaded previous BJP [Bharatiya Janata Party]—and Congress-led governments not to touch it.

Economist,
"Indian Women on the March,"
March 11, 2010. www.economist.com.

So, the first question I would like to raise is what policies do our politicians have to generate at least a million non-farm jobs every year for the next five years? Should not that question reign over corruption, criminalisation and the like? Will de-corruption and de-criminalisation create jobs of that order?

Decreased Demand

The problem India is facing is one of decreased demand—both in exports and also in local purchases, such as housing. There are still demands for education and health care as well as for water and energy that the country is unable to meet. As, in the immediate future, growth in exports is unlikely, the demand increase has to be raised from within.

If so, how can we do it? Do our economic policies help in meeting the existing demand and in creating fresh demand, too?

The fact remains that while the country has grown rapidly, disparities between the rich and the poor too [have] increased alarmingly. It should be a warning (unfortunately not much heeded) that Naxalite uprisings are greatest where disparities have increased most. Should we treat Naxalism as a problem of security or as a problem of unacceptable disparity?

In the prevailing circumstances, I suggest that what the Indian economy needs most is growth without increase in disparity, best done through faster increase in the incomes of the poor.

Two-Part Strategy

As a solution, economists are suggesting reduction in interest rates to enable private businesses to expand rapidly. Unfortunately, private businesses may use low-cost capital to build more houses for the rich, expand star hotels and such other artefacts that help the rich more than the poor.

Therefore, I suggest that what we need is a two-part strategy—low-cost capital to help the poor and a relatively high-cost strategy for the rich. Give low-interest loans only for activities such as rural development, schools, hospitals, water supply, energy and dwellings but leave the rest of the economy to be handled normally.

The government does provide these services in-house in government establishments. Unfortunately, in most cases, the quality of service leaves much to be desired. The costs are high but the quality is poor.

Hence, we need a system in which the state ensures that quality is good but prices are kept low by letting the purveyor have low-cost capital. The IITs, the NITs [National Institutes of Technology] and the Central Schools have enjoyed that facility but not the other services.

Here is a problem not of economics but one of governance. Governance is one of the issues repeatedly raised by the middle class. Regrettably, no political party in the country is talking of better governance.

Viewpoint 3

Zimbabwe Cannot Fully Democratize Until There Is Equal Distribution of Land and Resources

Baffour Ankomah

According to Baffour Ankomah in the following viewpoint, efforts by the West to promote democratic change in Zimbabwe have failed and have only reinforced the resistance of the regime to democratization. Until Zimbabwe solves issues related to land ownership, he contends, the country cannot be fully democratic. The best way to enact land reform is to allow Zimbabweans to work together to develop a common solution and redistribute land to poorer citizens. Ankomah is a Ghanaian journalist and the editor of New African.

As you read, consider the following questions:

1. According to the viewpoint, which United Nations official has misrepresented the need for the West to intervene in Zimbabwe?
2. Why did President Robert Mugabe seek reelection in 2008?
3. What is the name of the pro-presidential political party in Zimbabwe, according to Ankomah?

Baffour Ankomah, "The Core Issue in Zimbabwe," *New African*, August/September 2008, pp. 8–9.

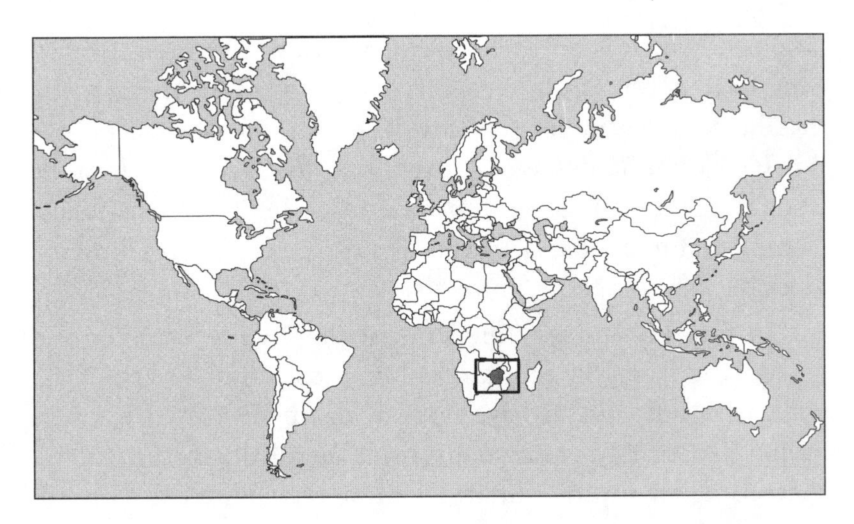

Many things have happened in Zimbabwe since the 29 March [2008] elections, in fact since the land issue exploded in 2000. I spent six weeks in Zimbabwe between 22 March and 13 July covering the recent elections, and so—on top of my eight years of intensive reporting of the country—I can say (if modesty should allow me) that I know a lot more than most "foreigners" do about Zimbabwe and what has gone on, and still going on, in that beautiful but besieged country. And I use the word "besieged" very advisedly.

Now that we are seeing a chink of light at the end of the Zimbabwean tunnel (via the recent inter-party dialogue), it is my turn to tell the world about some of the things we don't see on our TV screens or in the newspapers.

Western Interference

But first, something on Mark Malloch-Brown, ex-journalist, ex-UNDP [United Nations Development Programme] head, ex-right-hand man of [former secretary-general of the United Nations] Kofi Annan, and now the UK's [United Kingdom's] minister for Africa. He said at the height of the recent media campaign against Zimbabwe: "*We don't want it to be Zimbabwe versus Britain, it's Zimbabwe versus the world.*" Mark

Malloch-Brown is an ex-Rhodie (or former Rhodesian [referring to Rhodesia, an unrecognized state in South Africa]) who has made it big under the British system. We don't begrudge his steep rise, he deserves it even; but, for the life of him, he should stop creating the impression that he is a dispassionate commentator on Zimbabwean affairs. He is not! It's time he declared his competing interests.

In fact, his antics remind me of the English explorer and scientist of yore, Sir Francis Galton, a cousin of Charles Darwin, who was said to have been a "distinguished African explorer" (poor Africa, anybody could be distinguished there). According to my dictionary, Galton was "noted for his researches in heredity, meteorology, and statistics", and he even "founded the study of eugenics and the theory of anticyclones".

Well, the archives show that on 5 June 1873, Galton wrote a letter to the British daily, the *Times*, about what he wanted the Empire to do to Africa. "My proposal," he wrote, "is to make the encouragement of Chinese settlements of Africa a part of our national policy, in the belief that the Chinese immigrants would not only maintain their position, but that they would multiply and their descendants supplant the inferior Negro race. I should expect that the African seaboard, now sparsely occupied by lazy, palavering savages, might in a few years be tenanted by industrious, order-loving Chinese, living either as a semi-detached dependency of China, or else in perfect freedom under their own law". And yet, now that the Chinese are in Africa in full force and well ensconced in their comfortable villas and business houses all across the continent, the West is not happy. Recently, headlines such as the following have been appearing in the Western media: "*How China Is Taking over Africa . . . and Why We in the West Should be VERY Worried*".

Incidentally, "why we in the West should be very worried" is at the very core of the Zimbabwe saga; and anybody who wants to understand what is happening there, should pay serious attention to the core issue—what Mark Malloch-Brown cleverly calls "*Zimbabwe versus the world [nay the West]*".

In fact, the double veto by Russia and China at the UN [United Nations] Security Council on 11 July which effectively stopped what I call "the nations of European stock" from pushing Zimbabwe down a precipice, will, in the long run, be one of the best things to happen to the world this side of heaven. It is because of the double veto that [Zimbabwean prime minister] Morgan Tsvangirai ever signed the MoU [Memorandum of Understanding] paving the way for talks with the government, and even shook the hand of President [Robert] Mugabe for the first time since the formation of the MDC [political party, Movement for Democratic Change] in September 1999! The double veto has also given the power equation in the world a new vibrant colour—Anglo-Saxon United now knows that it cannot have its way all the time!

The core issue in Zimbabwe . . . is not a simple matter of democracy, good governance, human rights, hyperinflation and such like, but the land issue.

The Need for Land Reform

And here comes the rub: The core issue in Zimbabwe, despite what Western governments and their media say, is not a simple matter of democracy, good governance, human rights, hyperinflation and such like, but the land issue and the attempt by the Western powers—using local proxies—to stop a determined group of African people from asserting their inalienable rights over their country and resources (particularly the vexed land issue) because it sets a bad example for other nations in Africa and the developing world.

The fight, therefore, is for the soul of Zimbabwe and its resources, especially the land. And it is a direct fight between the Western powers on the one hand (Britain and America at the fore), and resolute Zimbabwean nationalists led by President Mugabe on the other hand.

This is why Mark Malloch-Brown could say: "*We don't want it to be Zimbabwe versus Britain, it's Zimbabwe versus the world*". Since when did an African country become "versus the world"? And for what exactly? The British weekly, the *Economist*, admits in a leader comment (headlined, "How to Get Him Out", 28 June 2008) that despite all the recent hyperactive coverage of Zimbabwe, "the loss of life in such blighted places as Sudan's Darfur province and Somalia is still many times higher than in Zimbabwe". And yet the magazine that prides itself as "the house journal of globalisation" still wants Mugabe kicked out! Until early July when the ICC [International Criminal Court] issued arrest warrants against Sudan's president, Omar al-Bashir, no one—and I mean no one—had said he should be kicked out because of Darfur where there has been far more loss of life than in Zimbabwe.

Sadly, the more the West interferes in Zimbabwe, the worse it becomes for the opposition.

In reality, the truth they dare not tell is that Anglo-Saxon United believes that if they can crush Zimbabwe, it will send a deafening message right across Africa and the developing world, and more especially in neighbouring South Africa and Namibia which have similar land tenure systems skewed in favour of their white minority populations, that any developing nation that dares to do a Zimbabwe will be doing so at its very peril. It is part of the control mechanism.

And anybody who does not understand this will never understand what is happening in Zimbabwe, and why this small African nation of 13 million people exercises so much fascination for the West and its media. Sadly, the more the West in-

Zimbabwe's Economic Troubles

The following table compares the key economic indicators of Zimbabwe in 2008 with the regional average.

Economic Indicators	Zimbabwe	Regional Average
Growth in Gross National Product	−3.6%	6%
Inflation	100,580%	9.5%
Unemployment	90%	30%
Percentage of population living below the national poverty line	80%	45%

TAKEN FROM: U.S. Central Intelligence Agency, *World Factbook, 2009*, 2010. https://www.cia.gov.

terferes in Zimbabwe, the worse it becomes for the opposition MDC. If the West had been wise and distanced itself a bit from the MDC and allowed it to grow as an organic local opposition, Tsvangirai may well be president by now.

The Role of President Mugabe

Even Mugabe would have stepped down as he planned to do when his 2002 presidential term ended in March 2008. For those who don't know, Mugabe had decided way back in late 2006 not to run in the 29 March elections! But attempts by Britain and its allies to humiliate him by trying to impose a regime change meant to reverse the land issue (including plotting a coup d'état last year), made him change his mind.

Even now if the West plays it wise, the 84-year-old president who wants to have time to write his books, might yet step down before his new five-year term ends in 2013. For those who can read between the lines, there are enough indications that Mugabe has prepared himself for this eventuality, even before the recent elections.

Take the new clause inserted in the constitution last year which says if a president does not finish his or her term, through retirement or death, the two houses of parliament will sit as a collegiate and elect a new president from within their midst. This clause replaced the old provision which said an election would be held within 90 days of a sitting president not finishing his or her term. The new clause is aimed at saving the country from the unnecessary pain of organising elections and the high costs associated with them.

The question is: Why does a sitting president agree to the insertion of such a clause in the constitution if he has no intention to step down before his term ends? But as long as the West continues to treat Zimbabwe in the way it has done in the last eight years, by imposing economic sanctions aimed at inducing regime change or making the people suffer so they will rise against the government, the nationalists in Zimbabwe will stiffen their resolve and stay put.

The Need for Internal Solutions

London, Washington, Paris, the EU [European Union] and the rest of Anglo-Saxon United should therefore wise up and back off, and allow the Zimbabweans (both opposition and government) to solve their own problems. If not, the West will find itself perpetually battling with nationalist steeliness in Zimbabwe to the detriment of the very same suffering people the West claims to want to help.

For a start, the West must lift the economic sanctions that they have imposed on Zimbabwe for the past eight years. The hypocritical antics of the same sanctions-imposing countries wanting the world to know that they have only imposed, or now want to impose, "targeted sanctions", "travel bans", and "assets freeze", will not help bring a solution in Zimbabwe. Who are they deceiving anyway?

London, Washington, Paris, the [European Union] and the rest of the Anglo-Saxon United should . . . back off, and allow the Zimbabweans (both opposition and government) to solve their own problems.

Before I sign off, let me hit on one of the things you didn't see on your TV screens or in your newspapers: The impression widely created by the Western media that the political violence in Zimbabwe was perpetrated by only one side—ZANU-PF [Zimbabwe African National Union-Patriotic Front] or "Mugabe's thugs"—is absolutely not true! The violence was perpetrated by both sides, ZANU-PF and MDC. There have been no saints in Zimbabwe! In fact, all independent analysts agree that it was the MDC that first started the violence, before ZANU-PF retaliated, and went on the offensive. Violence is violence, it is wrong, and should be condemned whoever perpetrates it.

Now that all three main parties have agreed to talk, let the world encourage them to go the full hog and find a lasting solution to the challenges facing the country. Anglo-Saxon United should stop trying to run the show by remote control and allow Tsvangirai to be (as he says) the "Zimbabwean who wants only what is best for our country and our citizens".

VIEWPOINT 4

Governments Must Maintain Capitalism to Preserve Democracy

Anatole Kaletsky

In this viewpoint, Anatole Kaletsky criticizes governments in the wake of the financial crisis that began in 2008. He contends that the governments of the United States and the United Kingdom undertook the wrong policies in an effort to capitalize on public dissatisfaction with large financial firms. Kaletsky also warns that citizens need to develop a better understanding of economics to avoid supporting policies that would undermine democracy. Kaletsky is an economist by training, who is also the editor-at-large and main economic contributor for the British newspaper the Times.

As you read, consider the following questions:

1. What does the author contend caused President Obama to convey "outrage"?
2. Who campaigned for "budgetary flexibility" and a rejection of the gold standard in the 1930s?
3. Which leading country's economy has continued to do well during the global economic contraction, according to Kaletsky?

Anatole Kaletsky, "Are Democracy and Capitalism Incompatible? Public Hatred of Bankers and Their Booty Stands in the Way of the Expansion Needed to Stop World Economic Collapse," *The Times* (London, England), March 29, 2009, p. 26.

Three weeks ago in his address to Congress [February 2009], President [Barack] Obama said: "In a time of crisis, we cannot afford to govern out of anger, or yield to the politics of the moment. I know how unpopular it is to be seen as helping banks when everyone is suffering from their bad decisions. But I also know that my job is to solve the problem."

What has happened—not only in America but also in Britain—to this promise of a calm, pragmatic response to the world's economic problems? This week Mr Obama expressed outrage at the $165 million bonuses paid by AIG [American International Group], the stricken insurance group, to executives in its financial products division who are responsible for most of its tens of billions of dollars in losses.

Britain and the Financial Crisis

In Britain the row over Sir Fred Goodwin's [the former head of the Royal Bank of Scotland] pension continues to grow. And in both countries, hatred of bankers is making it difficult for governments to take further action to stabilise the banks and support economic growth.

The behaviour of the bankers who first blew up the world financial system and then proceeded to loot it, is genuinely outrageous and deserves political retribution. But that should take the form of recovering the booty by the normal processes of law.

In Britain, the best approach would probably be for the Treasury and Financial Services Authority to launch civil lawsuits against Sir Fred and other senior bankers alleging negligence, breach of fiduciary duty and violation of numerous investment regulations by publishing misleading information about the financial condition of their companies.

Whether the Government would succeed in proving negligence is almost beside the point. The cost of the lawsuits alone, even if no damages were awarded, would be more than

"Blame It on the Poor," cartoon by Steve Greenberg, www.CartoonStock.com. Copyright © Steve Greenberg. Reproduction rights obtainable from www.CartoonStock.com.

enough to ruin most bankers. And even those rich enough to bear the financial costs of defending themselves would have their personal lives destroyed by being dragged through the courts.

This was the fate of the totally innocent directors of Equitable Life and of many guiltless members of Lloyd's.

Faced with the threat of such legal trauma, Sir Fred and the other "guilty men" of the banking community would have overwhelming incentives to reach out-of-court settlements—voluntarily giving up all their pensions and other gains in exchange for immunity from legal action.

U.S. Reaction

But such legal chess games do not satisfy lynch mobs—especially in America, where public fury is turning not only against individual bankers but against the system as a whole.

Even Democratic congressmen are now calling for the resignation of the Treasury Secretary, Tim Geithner, who has been in office for less than two months and is the only economic official confirmed so far by the Senate—and therefore quite literally the one man able to protect the country from total economic collapse.

This bloodlust raises a truly alarming question: Can capitalism and democracy survive side by side? Four months after Mr Obama's election the policy paralysis in Washington continues—and the backlash against the financial policies required to avert disaster becomes more vicious by the day.

This brings to mind a disconcerting historical reality airbrushed away in the simplified picture presented by textbook economics: The people who are now blamed for the Great Depression of the 1930s and Japan's lost decade—Andrew Mellon, the US Treasury Secretary in the early 1930s, and Yasushi Mieno, the governor of the Bank of Japan from 1989 to 1994—were not stupid, ignorant or wicked.

They were considered at the time the leading economists and financiers of their generation and were widely admired for their honesty and ethical standards. And they enjoyed widespread public support for their puritanical views about the virtues of saving, the dangers of creating future booms and the necessity of punishing and "purging" imprudent and unethical boom-time behaviour.

Four months after Mr Obama's election the policy paralysis continues—and the backlash against the financial policies required to avert disaster becomes more vicious by the day.

The confusion of moralism and economics led to disaster, as even schoolchildren are now taught. But many people also understood this in the 1930s.

John Maynard Keynes [an economist] campaigned for budgetary flexibility and abandonment of the gold standard for at least a decade before publishing his General Theory

[*The General Theory of Employment, Interest and Money*] in 1936. And he was a genius of rhetoric as well as of economics. He could argue far more eloquently for expansionary policies than any of his latter-day disciples, from [Bank of England governor] Mervyn King and [Federal Reserve Chairman] Ben Bernanke down to humble journalistic scribblers such as myself.

He could explain his ideas with equal brilliance in the abstractions of Treasury mandarins or the straightforward language of common people: "Housewives of England, for every shilling you save, you put a man out of work for a day." But Keynes's arguments were ignored by democratic governments the world over. [British Prime Minister] Gordon Brown describes a document in the Treasury archives in which Keynes's proposals for saving Britain from depression were dismissed by the Permanent Secretary with three scribbled words: "Inflation, Extravagance, Bankruptcy." Most people in the 1930s agreed with the Treasury that Keynes was irresponsible and deluded. And that is what many believe today—that a debt crisis cannot be cured by borrowing; that saving is virtuous while spending is wasteful; that printing money creates inflation and that the best response to recession is to fire government bureaucrats.

The Dangers to Democracy

If these beliefs become conventional wisdom among voters, then coping with the economic crisis will become as difficult as it was in the 1930s—at least for democracies. And here we come to the real horror.

In the 1930s only one country put expansionary policies fully into practice. [Adolf] Hitler's Germany, guided by the explicitly Keynesian economic thinking of its Finance Minister, Hjalmar Schacht, rapidly restored full employment by building the autobahns, even before it turned to rearmament.

The US and Britain, by contrast, never applied expansionary policies, even in Roosevelt's New Deal. It took Hitler's war to create the consensus required for the bold fiscal policies that pulled the democratic countries out of depression.

Now consider this: Is it coincidence that China is [the] only leading economy where growth seems assured and there is no doubt about the solidity of the banking system? So, is democracy incompatible with bold economic expansion? Obviously, I hope this is not true—and I am encouraged that for 250 years everyone who has bet against American democracy and capitalism has lost. But what if President Obama proves unable to unify America around an effective policy to pull itself out of recession? I can think of only one answer: We had better start learning Chinese.

VIEWPOINT 5

The Persian Gulf States Enjoy Free Market Capitalism Without Democracy

Jean-Francois Seznec

In the following viewpoint, Jean-Francois Seznec argues that despite economic freedom, the countries of the Persian Gulf have limited political freedom. The rulers in the region promote free market capitalism because of its economic benefits, but retain a high level of political control over the populations. Nonetheless, by sharing economic wealth, the rulers are able to maintain a degree of stability. Seznec is a visiting professor at the Center for Contemporary Arab Studies at Georgetown University in Washington, D.C.

As you read, consider the following questions:

1. Which of the Gulf states is rated the most free by Freedom House?
2. What percentage of the world's chemicals and fertilizers are produced in the region, according to Seznec?
3. According to the viewpoint, what percentage of Saudis own stocks?

Jean-Francois Seznec, "Market Economy Without Democracy in the Gulf," Ameri ca.gov, June 11, 2008. Reproduced by permission of the author.the Gulf Cooperation

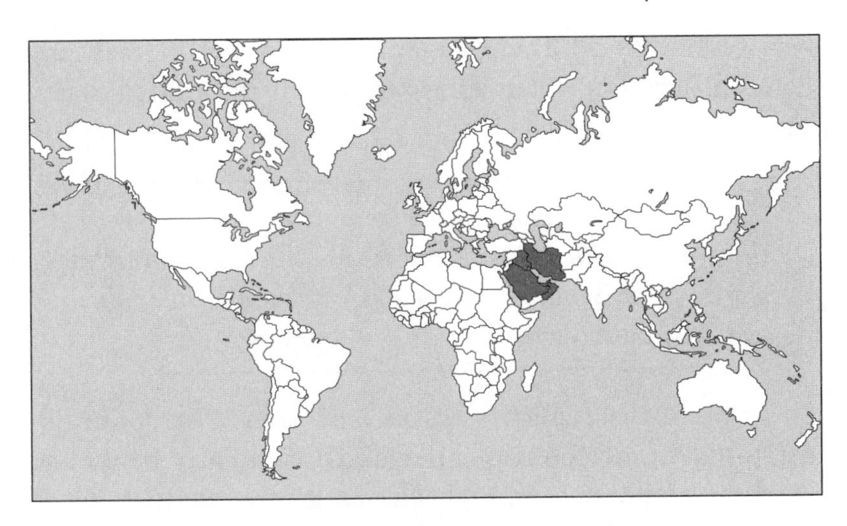

Market economies seem to thrive in certain nondemocratic states and yet do not seem to move these countries towards democracy. Consider the six countries that form Council (GCC): Bahrain, Kuwait, Oman, Qatar, Saudi Arabia, and the United Arab Emirates.

Wealth Without Freedom

On the Freedom House scale from 1 to 7 of freedom in the world, with 1 being the freest, the Gulf countries score poorly. Saudi Arabia gets 6.5 because of its limited civil and political rights. Highest scoring is Kuwait with only 4.0. Kuwait does have freely contested elections to parliament and freedom of expression, but the primacy of the royal family is not questioned.

By some measures, however, the Gulf states are among the freest markets in the world.

All Gulf countries are market economies. Saudi Arabia ranks a relatively high 23rd on the World Bank's list of countries for ease of doing business. All GCC countries are members of the World Trade Organization (WTO). Oman and Bahrain have free trade agreements with the United States. Tariffs are low.

On the Freedom House scale from 1 to 7 of freedom in the world, with 1 being the freest, the Gulf countries score poorly. Saudi Arabia gets 6.5 because of its limited civil and political rights.

None of the countries has income taxes. Corruption for day-to-day transactions is minimal. GCC country banks and financial institutions are sophisticated lenders. Restrictions on the sale of goods are limited, except for religiously forbidden products such as pork and alcohol.

The Gulf states also are modernizing their economic structures and laws to attract private investments, both local and foreign. Today a foreign company can own 100 percent of all its ventures in most GCC countries. It can repatriate its profits freely, sell assets as it wishes, and pay relatively low corporate taxes.

The Gulf countries' economies are booming. Moving to become less dependent on oil or gas, they are seeking to maximize their advantages of low-cost energy, plentiful capital, and strategic location. They already produce about 12 percent of all the world's chemicals and fertilizers. They are increasingly producing more advanced chemicals such as ethylene-based plastics. With access to cheap electricity, they are already large producers of aluminum, and, with future access to bauxite in Saudi Arabia, they may achieve 20 percent of world production before 2020.

Limits on Free Markets

Adherence to free markets has limits, of course. Contracts are not easy to enforce because of different legal traditions and few judges with knowledge of international legal practice.

In order to achieve economic development, the Gulf countries are investing hundreds of billions of dollars in infrastructure projects, building industrial cities, railroads, harbors, and airports.

Most of the very large chemical and metals companies operating in the GCC today are state owned, although managed like large Western companies with minimal interference from government. SABIC [Saudi Basic Industries Corp.], for example, is the most profitable and fastest-growing chemical company in the world with access to raw materials at the lowest cost. It is also becoming a research and development powerhouse and, like its petroleum counterpart, Saudi Aramco, trains and uses Saudis to create knowledge-based industries in the kingdom.

In order to achieve economic development, the Gulf countries are investing hundreds of billions of dollars in infrastructure projects, building industrial cities, railroads, harbors, and airports.

The success of state-owned companies has drawbacks. Managers insist they should not have to share their low-cost raw materials with local competitors. Thus, while very large state enterprises create work for the private-market economy, they also restrict private-sector competitors from getting too large.

Of course, some interests in the GCC resist free markets, including traditional manufacturers and merchants. The religiously conservative Salafis [those who use a strict interpretation of Islam] also lobby against free markets, fearing that an open economy invites widespread Western-style education and practices.

Democracy and Terrorism

Since the attacks of September 11, 2001, Americans have struggled to articulate an overarching, long-term strategy for fighting religious extremism and terror in the Middle East. Most experts on both the Left and Right agree that promoting democracy will help address the root causes of terrorism in the region, though they differ on to what degree. The reasoning is simple: If Arabs and Muslims lack legitimate, peaceful outlets with which to express their grievances, they are more likely to resort to violence. In one important 2003 study, Princeton University's Alan Krueger and Czech scholar Jitka Maleckova analyzed extensive data on terrorist attacks and concluded that "the only variable that was consistently associated with the number of terrorists was the Freedom House index of political rights and civil liberties. Countries with more freedom were less likely to be the birthplace of international terrorists."

Shadi Hamid, "Engaging Political Islam to Promote Democracy," Progressive Policy Institute, Policy Report, June 2007. www.ppionline.org.

Sharing Wealth, Not Power

To achieve their ambitious economic goals, the governments of the Gulf have sought to share wealth, but not political power, with their people.

Saudi authorities have used the stock market to share the wealth. Many of the 115 companies listed are controlled by the state and are usually very profitable; these companies will sell perhaps 30 percent of their capital as stock market shares. Saudis who invest in these state-owned companies get good dividends and capital appreciation on safe investments. Furthermore, the Capital Markets Authority ensures that all the companies listed are bona fide and that small investors get a chance to buy shares. Today 50 percent of all Saudis own shares and hence have a stake in the development of the kingdom.

Gulf governments fear, however, that sharing political power with their people could bring development to a screeching halt. The few freely held elections in the Gulf have given absolute majorities to the Salafis. To balance Salafi gains, GCC kings and emirs have appointed consultative councils, comprising technocrats who give a stamp of participatory approval to economic policy and uncontroversial laws.

Lack of judicial independence demonstrates another divide in the Gulf states between sharing wealth and political power. Government-appointed judges rule in cases of Islamic family and criminal law but lack competence in commercial law. The Saudis have established a parallel legal system called the Board of Grievances to handle commercial cases.

Yet the powerful remain beyond the reach of the courts. The Saudi Board of Grievances does not consider disputes involving princes and government officials; rarely are such cases adjudicated on merit.

Growth of free markets, both promoted and hampered by autocracy, has done little to effect political reform in the Gulf states. The free market economies are sustained by the unquestioned political control of their leaders. Even in Dubai [in the United Arab Emirates], the entrepreneurial center of the region, the word of the ruler is the rule of the land.

The Gulf governments are not of the people, by the people, for the people. They are governments of the few for the benefits of the many. This is a far cry from what Western democracies have achieved, but it is homegrown.

Democracy cannot be imposed from the outside. Ongoing economic changes in the Gulf may be indicating that, over time, the rulers there will allow not only market freedom but also political freedoms such as political parties, free speech, and independence of an educated judiciary. Ultimately, promoting economic participation and reform may still promote democracy.

Malaysia's Citizens Demand Democracy with Development

Francis Loh

In the following viewpoint, Francis Loh presents an overview of Malaysia's problems balancing economic development and democracy. Major issues in the country have been corruption and efforts to investigate and curb abuse. The author presents a number of examples of corruption and explores why efforts to reform have been constrained by the country's political system. Loh is a professor at the Science University of Malaysia and secretary for the Malaysian democracy group Aliran.

As you read, consider the following questions:

1. Who was found dead after being interviewed by the Malaysian Anti-Corruption Commission, according to Loh?
2. Which Malaysian prime minister has renewed economic development in the country?
3. How have federal departments reacted to some activities of the state governments, according to the viewpoint?

On 21 August 2009, a 'Forum Perdana' was held in the Kompleks Masyarakat Penyayang, Penang, to honour Teoh Beng Hock, who was found dead after having been interrogated by the Malaysian Anti-Corruption Commission (MACC) for more than 10 hours (beginning from 5:00 P.M. on 15 July

Francis Loh, "We Demand Development and Democracy," Aliran, October 2, 2009. Reproduced by permission.

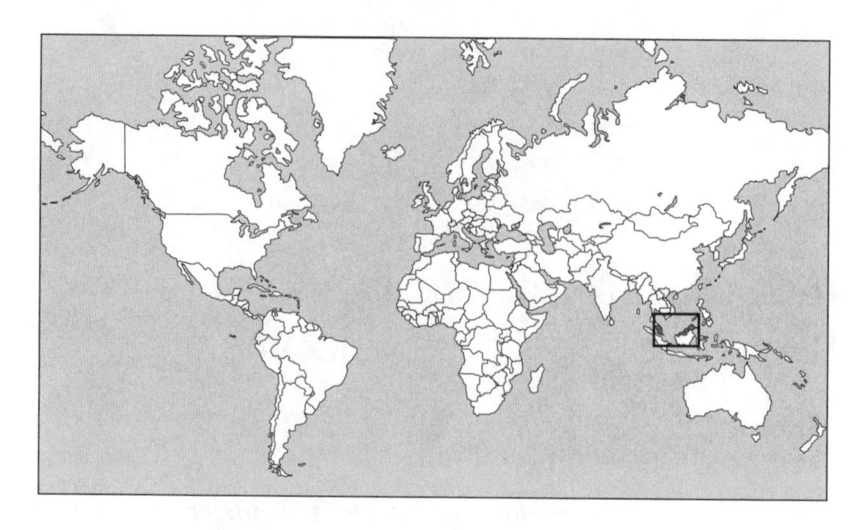

to 3:45 A.M. the next day). Teoh, a political aide to Ean Yong Hian Wah, a Selangor State Exco member, was found on the fifth-floor rooftop of Plaza Masalam, which also houses the Selangor MACC, nine floors above.

The forum was also an opportunity to discuss the circumstances that led to Teoh's interrogation, namely, a concerted effort by the MACC to look into the alleged misuse of constituency development funds by DAP [Democratic Action Party] and PKR [Parti Keadilan Rakyat] elected assembly members in Selangor. The forum called for the setting up of a Royal Commission of Inquiry to investigate Teoh's death.

The fact that the forum could be organised at such short notice, and in a government facility like the Kompleks Penyayang, which traditionally was out-of-bounds to opposition parties, speaks volumes for the fact that the Barisan Nasional (BN) is no longer governing Penang. Instead, it is the Pakatan Rakyat (PR) that is now in charge, hence the ease in accessing the Kompleks. In the event, the hall upstairs, which can sit about 2,000 people, was filled to capacity. An equally large mass of people gathered in the foyer downstairs, some seated, the majority standing, watching a giant screen, which relayed to these people the proceedings being conducted upstairs. All in all about 5,000 people were present. Similar public meetings including a vigil in front of the Selangor MACC building were also held.

Hopefully, Malaysians shall recognise the political significance of Teoh's death. Now that the prime minister Datuk Seri Najib Tun Razak has promised to set up a Royal Commission of Inquiry (RCI), following the completion of the ongoing inquest into Teoh's death, and notwithstanding popular criticism of the limited terms of reference set for the RCI, there will be opportunity to discuss publicly the workings of the MACC. Newly set up during Abdullah Badawi's tenure as prime minister, amidst considerable hype that the MACC, unlike its predecessor would be more autonomous and have greater investigative powers, it appears that the MACC's impartiality and credibility have been compromised in the eyes of many Malaysians.

In one instance, a [Barisan Nasional] assemblyman had spent almost RM500,000 [$156,568] in Selangor state allocations in 44 days just prior to the 2008 election!

The Credibility of the Government

Malaysians are asking why the MACC is chasing after DAP and PKR elected assembly members in Selangor over alleged misuse of quite 'mosquito' amounts of constituency development funds. The explanation offered by the MACC's deputy commissioner is that complaints have been filed against these PR politicians. If that be the case, what then has happened to the complaints that were filed by PR politicians and other concerned Malaysians in 2008 against previous BN assembly members for the same kind of offences? In one instance, a BN assemblyman had spent almost RM500,000 [$156,568] in Selangor state allocations in 44 days just prior to the 2008 election!

Complaints were also filed against the former assembly members of Kampung Tunku, Kajang and Taman Medan. A media item on 29 July 2009 further reported two cases of suspected fraud uncovered in two Village Development and Security Committees (JKKK) by the Selangor executive councilor in charge of the JKKKs. He had filed reports against the two erring JKKKs several months ago. Yet, in contrast to its investigations into the PR assembly members, the MACC does not appear to be acting with the same lightning speed on these earlier cases involving BN politicians.

Significantly, the MACC has also stated that it might be investigating 'graft allegations published in a blog against Selangor executive council members Ronnie Liu and Ean Yong Hian Wah . . . even without a report being lodged by the public'. For 'if there is a basis for the allegation, a MACC officer may lodge a report with us, thus enabling an investigation'.

If this be the case, the MACC must also investigate how the former Selangor Menteri Besar Dr Mohd Khir Toyo was able to finance the building of his multi-million ringgit [Malaysian currency] house. After all, the MACC had earlier—again with lightning speed—investigated the complaint that current Selangor [Menteri Besar] Tan Sri Khalid Ibrahim had allegedly committed corruption in the purchase of 46 cows for his constituency and that he had used state funds to maintain his personal car.

However, it is hoped that Teoh's passing will give Malaysians more food for thought than simply asking questions about the MACC's impartiality. It is hoped that Malaysians will pause and reflect about the overall conduct of politics in Malaysia. For it appears that too much emphasis is being given to development issues, too little attention to issues of democratisation.

For it appears that too much emphasis is being given to development issues, too little attention to issues of democratisation.

Focus on Development

It is not surprising that Malaysians have focused on issues of development rather than on democratising our politics; after all a global economic crisis is looming. President [Barack] Obama, the EEC [European Economic Community] leaders and Prime Minister Aso Taro of Japan have all focused attention on the economic crisis too.

Moreover, as I have argued on other occasions, there exists a culture of developmentalism among Malaysians, one that has prioritised rapid economic growth above other values, including democracy. So the emphasis given to issues of economic development by BN leaders and the BN-controlled media, especially following Najib's takeover as Malaysia's sixth prime minister, has caused ordinary Malaysians to become more engrossed with development issues once again.

For many ordinary Malaysians, Najib, in contrast to his predecessor Datuk Seri Abdullah [Haji Admad] Badawi, seems to have given a new impetus to economic development and a sense of dynamism to the country. In order to kick-start the economy at a time of global economic slowdown, Najib first removed previous bumiputera participation requirements in the service sector in order to attract foreign investors. He has also promised to revamp the much-abused Approved Permits import scheme which privileged certain individuals and companies with connections to people in high places.

This latest economic initiative . . . is expected to generate investments worth RM90 billion [$28.2 billion] and create 220,000 new jobs by 2020.

Other related moves were to launch a new pension scheme for the private sector and to offer for sale 20 billion units of Amanah Saham 1Malaysia trust funds for sale to all Malaysians. No doubt, when these initiatives are fully in place, there will be more funds to invest in the local stock market while the Malaysian economy as a whole might become more competitive.

In late July [2009], with much fanfare he also launched the first Special Economic Zone (SEZ) with the aim of boosting investments and creating jobs in the east coast of peninsular Malaysia, stretching from Kerteh, Terengganu, in the north to Pekan, Pahang, in the south which is incidentally Najib's hometown and electoral constituency. The local media has hyped up this latest economic initiative that is expected to generate investments worth RM90 billion [$28.2 billion] and create 220,000 new jobs by 2020.

Predictably, the business community has welcomed the setting up of the SEZ and Najib's other economic policies especially since investors have been promised special incentives including tax exemption for ten years. (That said, it remains unclear how this SEZ will relate to the East Coast Economic Region corridor development plan as contained in the Ninth Malaysia Plan and launched by Abdullah earlier.)

The Role of State Governments

The flip side to the excitement over Najib's economic initiatives has been growing concern among ordinary Malaysians over the economic performance of the PR governments. It is

Corruption in Malaysia

Rooting out corruption is more complex [in Malaysia] than in neighboring countries like Thailand or Indonesia ... because corruption is not an appendage to the system. In some ways, it is the system....

"In a Western context, [a program of affirmative action for its majority ethnic group, the Malays] is regarded as ... undue preference which is a form of corruption," said Ramon Navaratnam, a former top official at the Malaysian Finance Ministry.

Thomas Fuller, "Malaysia's Crackdown on Corruption Has Its Skeptics," New York Times, *May 2, 2006. www.nytimes.com.*

fair to say that nothing spectacular has occurred on this front, often, in spite of the best efforts of the PR governments. Worse, there have been many complaints that voting in a PR government has not led to any noticeable improvement in the realm of development. For instance, there was much concern in Selangor and Penang that the state government had allowed building projects in steep hill slopes (that contravened the 2002 guidelines of the Ministry of Science and Environment), which had been approved by the previous BN governments, to go ahead instead of halting them.

Let me focus on some major criticisms that have been hurled at the PR government in Penang. Due to this reluctance to arrest such steep hillslope projects, severe mudslides had occurred in several parts of Tanjung Bungah and along the Tanjung Bungah-Batu Ferringhi coastal road resulting in much inconvenience for residents and road users, financial losses, and threats to lives.

The Tanjung Bungah Residents' Association (TBRA) has been particularly vocal on this matter and had lobbied the local authority to issue the necessary 'stop work order' against the responsible developers. Although such orders were issued belatedly, blasting and land development work has continued, which led the TBRA to accuse the authorities of a sheer lack of serious monitoring of the situation, and also insinuating that perhaps corruption was involved.

A related complaint, also by the TBRA, was over the state government's approval of more high-rise projects on the beachfront. There was general agreement between the two parties that higher densities were allowed in Penang's 'first corridor' and that there would be lower densities allowed in the 'second corridor'. The disagreement arose due to differences over where the boundary between the two corridors stood. As a result of the Penang state government's delineation of that boundary beyond Tanjung Bungah village, there will now be even more 41-storey high-rises on the Tanjung Bungah beachfront.

Another complaint that made the headlines concerned the proposed construction of four new high-rise buildings in the heritage zone of Georgetown which threatened to jeopardise the city's recent acquisition of Unesco [United Nations Educational, Scientific and Cultural Organization] world heritage status. Of these four projects, three had been approved by the previous BN government while a fourth was approved by the new PR government. Although the chief minister, Lim Guan Eng, finally imposed the necessary height limits and ordered all four developers concerned to scale down their projects accordingly, the Penang Heritage Trust [a nongovernmental organization] argued that the PR state government should have acted more decisively in the first instance.

And of course, there has been much criticism over the state government's inability or reluctance to invoke certain provisions in the land laws to reverse the acquisition of Kg

Buah Pala or High Chaparral by the Koperasi Pegawai Kerajaan Negeri Pulau Pinang. The cooperative, along with the developer, Nusmetro Ventures Sdn Bhd, is planning to evict the Indian community there who are able to trace their roots back to three to four generations. Although the approval of the project was concluded before the PR state government came to power, and in spite of its various attempts to resolve the matter, criticism of the PR government persisted, not least because many outsiders—Hindraf [Hindu Rights Action Force], MIC [Malaysian Indian Congress], the federal government, and the former chief minister, Koh Tsu Koon—appeared to be forcing the issue.

The upshot of all these is that the Penang state government stands accused of being too friendly to the developers and not concerned enough about ordinary people, the environment and heritage—not unlike how many perceived the previous BN government. Why bother, therefore, to push for change if things don't change at all?

Political Constraints

While these are pertinent criticisms, it is important to keep in mind the larger political picture as well. In fact, political constraints had circumscribed the development capacity of the PR state governments. In defence of the PR state governments, three explanations might be offered.

First, is the problem of a politicised bureaucracy. Having served under a BN government for more than 50 years, it was predictable that the federal, state and even the local government bureaucracies would be uncooperative, sometimes hostile, towards the PR executives. This was particularly true of PTD (Administrative and Diplomatic Service) officers who were appointed to top positions in the state bureaucracy by the federal government. PR leaders have complained about the heads of their legal, financial, land and mines, and Islamic affairs departments, the local authority bosses as well as district officers, who posed all kinds of problems to the new governments. In some cases, fortunately, the new PR governments have been able to appoint PTD officers of their own choice, upon the retirement or transfer of incumbent officers.

But this is only one aspect of the problem. For as a result of the politicisation of the bureaucracy, slack and incompetence have crept in. Numerous officers who are not competent have been promoted on account of their loyalty to the BN. It follows that they cannot be competent supervisors of lower echelon civil servants. This is no secret! The point is that politicisation has resulted not only in a pro-BN bureaucracy, but one that is riddled with incompetency as well. Hence it is not surprising that even when 'stop work orders' have been issued, developers dare to continue with their activities.

Apart from this, the state bureaucracy operates alongside the federal one that only takes orders from the federal ministries. The relationship between the PR-state governments and the departments of education, consumer affairs, MIDA [Malaysian Industrial Development Authority], even health, tourism, culture and welfare have remained tense even now, more than 17 months after the change of government. The lightning speed with which the MACC, a federal agency, has conducted itself vis-à-vis the allegations of corruption among PR politicians is a reminder of this polarisation between the federal and the state authorities.

It was predictable that the federal, state and even the local government bureaucracies would be uncooperative, sometimes hostile.

Moreover, activities organised by state governments have been boycotted by these federal departments too. And since the federal departments have access to more funds than do their state counterparts, the federal departments often organise their own functions and projects to outdo those conducted by the latter, often in the same areas.

Second, the PR state governments are hampered by a dire shortage of development funds. Under the Federal Constitution, the federal government has sole jurisdiction over the disbursement of development funds. It is only obliged to provide two major grants to the state governments, namely the 'capitation grant' which is based on the population size, and the 'state road grant', which helps the state to maintain their network of roads but which is in effect a grant that takes into consideration the geographical size of the state.

Apart from these two grants, there are about 10 other shared taxes and levies that the state is allowed to collect or where the federal government has to reimburse the state. In a state like Penang, which has very little access to land and forest, and does not possess any petroleum or mineral resources, all of which fall under the purview of the state, the total revenue raised by the state is small and can only cover operating expenditure. Hardly any funds are left for development purposes!

In the 'Restructuring and Reshaping Penang' conference held in June 2009, two distinguished economists revealed that the Penang state government's annual budget is less than half that of Universiti Sains Malaysia's [the Science University of Malaysia's], which became flushed with funds after being awarded 'apex' status. The point is that the economic performance of the PR governments, especially that of the Penang government, has been severely handicapped by a dire shortage of funds under the centralised system of fiscal federalism, which characterises Malaysia. No doubt, a fairer redistribution of development funds to the states must be at the top of the PR's agenda, if and when they come to power in Putrajaya.

And third, it is most unfortunate for the PR state governments that they have come to power in the midst of a global economic crisis, for which they are not responsible. As well, in many instances, a large proportion of the state executive councillors have very limited capacity in handling economic problems. Many of the more experienced PR politicians who have a better grasp of issues of governance, including dealing with the politicised bureaucracy, are not involved in the PR state governments. For they had contested for parliamentary seats rather than for state assembly ones. It has therefore been a fast learning curve for the less experienced, often first time, politicians appointed to executive councillor posts. Given the global economic crisis, the politicised bureaucracy, the lack of development allocations to the state, many of the PR state governments have underperformed.

Periodical Bibliography

The following articles have been selected to supplement the diverse views presented in this chapter.

Leslie Elliott Armijo and Carlos Gervasoni — "Two Dimensions of Democracy and the Economy," *Democratization*, February 2010.

Beijing Review — "Is the Divided Fiscal Seal a Symbol of Democracy?" January 10, 2008.

Jorge Castañeda and Patricio Navia — "Of Democracy & Dinero," *National Interest*, July–August 2008.

Daniel Griswold — "Trade, Democracy and Peace: The Virtuous Cycle," Cato Institute, April 20, 2007. www.cato.org.

Taras Kuzio — "Opinion: President Yanukovych Threatens Ukraine's Democracy," *GlobalPost*, April 12, 2010.

Hunter Lewis — "Transforming Capitalism: Worker-Owned Business, or Expanding the Non-Profit Sector?" *World Watch*, January–February 2010.

Jack Mintz — "Democracy Power," *Canadian Business*, July 20, 2009.

Rein Müllerson — "Democratisation Through the Supply-Demand Prism," *Human Rights Review*, November 2009.

Alina Mungiu-Pippidi — "The Other Transition," *Journal of Democracy*, January 2010.

David Ransom — "Globalization on the Rocks," *New Internationalist*, March 2010.

Paul Wells — "A Losing Battle," *Maclean's*, February 12, 2010.

Richard Wike — "Hungary Dissatisfied with Democracy, but Not Its Ideals," Pew Research Center, April 7, 2010. http://pewresearch.org.

CHAPTER 4

Democracy and International Relations

Viewpoint 1

The United States Should Lead by Example to Promote Democracy Around the World

Joseph Nye

In the following viewpoint, Joseph Nye argues that the George W. Bush administration's policies undermined U.S. efforts to promote democracy abroad. Specifically, the author contends that actions such as the invasion of Iraq led many to perceive U.S. pro-democracy efforts as a new form of imperialism. Meanwhile, efforts to protect Americans from terrorism were seen as erosions of liberty within the United States. Nye is a world-renowned scholar and a professor of international relations at Harvard University.

As you read, consider the following questions:

1. What are the "three Ds" of American foreign policy under President Barack Obama?
2. How much did the number of countries rated as "free" by Freedom House increase during the presidency of George W. Bush?
3. According to Nye, what happens in democracies during periods of "extreme fear"?

Joseph Nye, "Joseph Nye Commentary: Taking Democracy to the People," *Globe & Mail*, May 13, 2009. Copyright © 2009 Globe Interactive, a division of Bell Globemedia Publishing, Inc. Reproduced by permission.

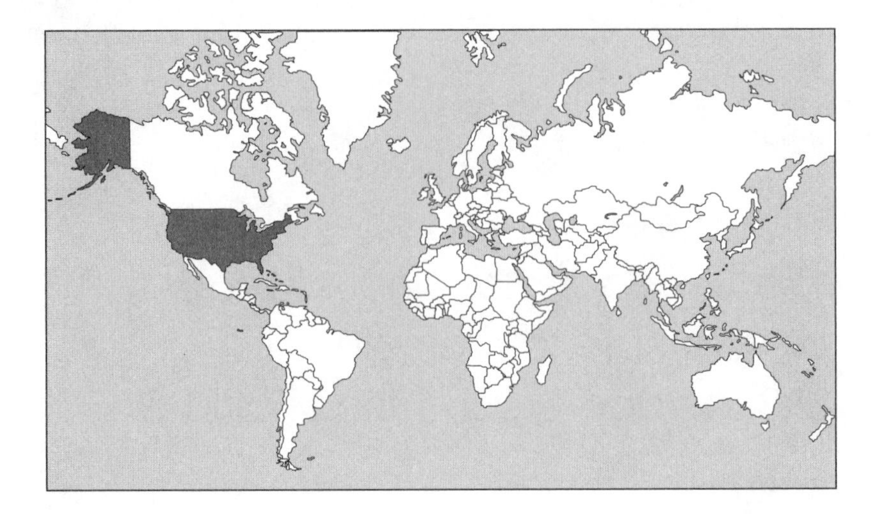

U.S. president George W. Bush was famous for proclaiming the promotion of democracy a central focus of American foreign policy. He was not alone in this rhetoric. Most presidents since Woodrow Wilson have made similar statements.

So it was striking when Secretary of State Hillary Clinton testified to Congress earlier this year about the "three Ds" of U.S. foreign policy—defence, diplomacy, development. The "D" of democracy was noticeable by its absence, suggesting a change in policy by Barack Obama's administration.

Both [former president] Bill Clinton and Mr. Bush frequently referred to the beneficial effects of democracy on security. They cited social-science studies showing that democracies rarely go to war with each other. But, more carefully stated, what scholars show is that liberal democracies almost never go to war with each other, and it may be that a liberal constitutional culture is more important than the mere fact of elections.

What Is a Democracy?

While elections are important, liberal democracy is more than "electocracy." Elections in the absence of constitutional and cultural constraints can produce violence, as in Bosnia or the Palestinian Authority. And illiberal democracies have fought each other, as Ecuador and Peru did in the 1990s.

In the eyes of many critics at home and abroad, the Bush administration's excesses tarnished the idea of democracy promotion. Mr. Bush's invocation of democracy to justify the invasion of Iraq implied that democracy could be imposed at the barrel of a gun. The word democracy came to be associated with its particular American variant, and took on an imperialist connotation.

Elections in the absence of constitutional and cultural constraints can produce violence, as in Bosnia or the Palestinian Authority. And illiberal democracies have fought each other, as Ecuador and Peru did in the 1990s.

Moreover, Mr. Bush's exaggerated rhetoric was often at odds with his practice, giving rise to charges of hypocrisy. It was far easier for him to criticize Zimbabwe, Cuba and Myanmar than Saudi Arabia and Pakistan, and his initial criticism of Egypt was soon toned down.

There is a danger, however, in overreacting to the failures of the Bush administration's policies. The growth of democracy is not an American imposition, and it can take many forms. The desire for greater participation is widespread as economies develop and people adjust to modernization. Democracy is not in retreat. Freedom House, a nongovernmental organization, listed 86 free countries at the beginning of the Bush years, and a slight increase to 89 by the end of his term.

Democracy remains a worthy and widespread goal, but it is important to distinguish the goal from the means used to attain it. There is a difference between assertive promotion and more gentle support of democratization. Avoiding coercion, premature elections and hypocritical rhetoric should not

> ### The Failure of Democratic Reforms in Ukraine
>
> [Pro-Western reformer Viktor] Yushchenko and his allies failed to make good on their promises of implementing democratic reforms, ending rampant corruption and creating a better quality of life. The stirring rhetoric of the revolution soon crashed against the sobering reality of Ukrainian politics, dominated since independence in 1991 by powerful business leaders and a deeply embedded system of patronage and graft.
>
> *James Marson, "In Ukraine, the Death of the Orange Revolution,"* Time, *February 3, 2010. www.time.com.*

preclude a patient policy that relies on economic assistance, behind-the-scenes diplomacy and multilateral approaches to aid the development of civil society, the rule of law and well-managed elections.

Equally important to the foreign-policy methods used to support democracy abroad are the ways in which it is practised in the United States. When Americans try to impose democracy, they tarnish it. When they live up to their own best traditions, they can stimulate emulation and create the soft power of attraction. This is what [President] Ronald Reagan called the "shining city on the hill."

International Opinion About U.S. Democracy

For example, many people both inside and outside the United States had become cynical about the American political system, arguing it was dominated by money and closed to outsiders. The election of Barack Hussein Obama in 2008 did a great deal to restore the soft power of American democracy.

Another aspect of America's domestic practice of liberal democracy that is currently being debated is how it deals with the threat of terrorism. In the climate of extreme fear that followed the 9/11 attacks [terrorist attacks of September 11, 2001], the Bush administration engaged in tortured legal interpretations of international and domestic law that tarnished American democracy and diminished its soft power.

Fortunately, a free press, an independent judiciary, and a pluralist legislature helped to hold such practices up for public debate. Mr. Obama has proclaimed that he will close the Guantánamo Bay detention facility within a year, and he has declassified the legal memos that were used to justify what is now widely regarded as torture of detainees.

But the problem of how to deal with terrorism is not just a matter of history. The threat remains, and it is important to remember that people in democracies want both liberty and security.

Democracy and Terrorism

In moments of extreme fear, the pendulum of attitudes swings toward the security end of that spectrum. [President] Abraham Lincoln suspended the right of habeas corpus—the principle that detainees are entitled to challenge their detention in a court of law—during the Civil War, and [President] Franklin Roosevelt interned Japanese-American citizens during the early days of the Second World War.

When some of the Bush administration's more reasonable members are asked today how they could have taken the positions they did in 2002, they cite the anthrax attacks that followed 9/11, the intelligence reports of an impending attack with nuclear materials, and the widespread fear of a second attack against the American people. In such circumstances, liberal democracy and security are in tension.

Terrorists hope to create a climate of fear and insecurity that will provoke us to harm ourselves by undercutting the quality of our own liberal democracy.

Terrorism is a form of theatre. It invokes its effects not by sheer destruction, but by dramatizing atrocious acts against civilians. Terrorism is like jiu-jitsu. The weaker adversary leverages the power of the stronger against itself.

Terrorists hope to create a climate of fear and insecurity that will provoke us to harm ourselves by undercutting the quality of our own liberal democracy. Preventing new terrorist attacks while understanding and avoiding the mistakes of the past will be essential if we are to preserve and support liberal democracy both at home and abroad. That is the debate that the Obama administration is leading in the United States today.

Viewpoint 2

Afghanistan Needs Security Before It Can Have Democracy

Gretchen Peters

In the following viewpoint, journalist Gretchen Peters contends that democracy cannot flourish in Afghanistan until widespread security exists. As an antigovernment and anti-Western insurgency has grown, people have lost confidence in the ruling regime and are increasingly hostile toward the international peacekeeping force in the country, led by the North Atlantic Treaty Organization (NATO). One of the main reasons for the insurgency, Peters asserts, has been the dissatisfaction of the dominant Pashtun ethnic groups with the post-Taliban regime. Peters is the author of Seeds of Terror, *a book about the drug trade and terrorism in Afghanistan.*

As you read, consider the following questions:

1. What group is leading the antigovernment insurgency in Afghanistan?
2. According to the viewpoint, what are the three main causes for "apathy" toward democratic elections among the Pashtun people?
3. What are the main challenges the Afghans faced in the August 2009 elections?

Gretchen Peters, "Afghanistan's Democracy Fatigue," *Foreign Policy*, March 2009.

When Afghanistan held presidential elections in 2004, Haji Kabeer, a 68-year-old villager from Helmand province, trekked to the polling booth, bringing along the women in his household.

"The Taliban had warned us not to," he said, "but we voted anyway, believing elections would bring us a better future."

Five years later, Kabeer can't see the point in taking the same risk again. His province has been the scene of vicious fighting between insurgents and NATO [North Atlantic Treaty Organization] troops, and he, like many villagers in the south, feels trapped in the middle of their battle. The Taliban has distributed night letters in his area, warning villagers of dire consequences for participating in the coming electoral process.

Moreover, he views the government of President Hamid Karzai as corrupt and ineffectual, and complains that democracy has brought no tangible improvements to his area, such as roads, schools, and health clinics.

"I am not voting for Karzai again; that's for sure," Kabeer said, adding that he knew few people in his tribe who planned to cast a ballot at all. "I doubt there will be a strong turnout in this area."

Kabeer expressed an oft heard sentiment across the country's southern and eastern provinces, where many Afghans feel let down by the democratic process. It's an attitude that should have the international community worried as it prepares to support what will surely be a complex and dangerous election process. For Afghanistan's presidential elections to be credible and their results accepted, all ethnic groups in every region of the country must feel included.

For Afghanistan's presidential elections to be credible and their results accepted, all ethnic groups in every region of the country must feel included.

Afghan Elections

In recent weeks, the Afghan capital has been embroiled in a debate over when Afghanistan should hold its presidential election. Now that the Election Commission has officially set the polling date for Aug. 20 [2009], opposition leaders are calling for Karzai to step down when his official term ends in May. The constitutional crisis has consumed Kabul's [capital of Afghanistan] political elite and dominated media coverage, thus disguising the wider dilemma in the country's troubled and predominantly Pashtun south. There, many ordinary Afghans are wondering why another round of elections is being held at all.

Indifference among Pashtuns, and in many cases, an outright hostility toward the entire voting process, stands in stark contrast to the widespread optimism felt ahead of the October 2004 presidential vote, when millions of Afghans from across the country's ethnic spectrum lined up to cast their ballots, even in remote districts of the Pashtun south where UN [United Nations] organizers feared low turnout.

Although the [Barack] Obama administration has tried to lower expectations, at least domestically, for what it hopes to achieve in Afghanistan, there nonetheless remains broad support for Afghanistan to continue its experiment with democracy, now enshrined in the country's Constitution. Many political analysts argue that the custom of holding elections, even if some early rounds may be somewhat flawed, eventually builds a stable democratic foundation.

"If one were to move away from the electoral process at this moment, a major constitutional crisis would occur," said William Maley, an expert on Afghanistan at the Australian National University. "If it came from Karzai it would be seen as a power grab, and if it came from anywhere else it would be rejected by political leaders in the north and west who would say, 'We have got our act together; why can't the Pashtuns?'"

It's fair to say that many Afghans had unrealistic expectations for their country's swift turnaround. Yet it is critical, as the international community and the United States in particular seek to forge a new direction in Afghanistan, to take note of why many Pashtuns have become so disgusted so quickly with the democratic process.

"So many promises were made, but so little was done," said Khalid Khan, a medical student in eastern Nangarhar province. "People have lost faith in the idea of voting."

It's fair to say that many Afghans had unrealistic expectations for their country's swift turnaround.

Apathy among Pashtuns stems from three overlapping concerns: poor security across the south and east, disenchantment with the Karzai government and NATO, and a growing sense that their ethnic group will be disenfranchised in the polls.

Terrorism and Insurgency

Insecurity in the south forced the Independent Election Commission (IEC) to briefly delay registering voters in the four

Coalition Military Fatalities in Afghanistan

Year	US	UK	Other	Total
2001	12	0	0	12
2002	49	3	17	69
2003	48	0	9	57
2004	52	1	7	60
2005	99	1	31	131
2006	98	39	54	191
2007	117	42	73	232
2008	155	51	89	295
2009	317	108	96	521
2010	174	53	42	269
Total	1121	298	418	1837

Total fatalities as of June 18, 2010.

TAKEN FROM: iCasualties.org, "Coalition Military Fatalities by Year," June 18, 2010. http://www.icasualties.org.

provinces where the Taliban insurgency is strongest. So far, the IEC has managed to register just over half a million people in Helmand, Kandahar, Nimroz, and Uruzgan combined, an IEC spokesperson said, or about 1 million fewer people than were registered in those provinces ahead of the presidential vote in 2004.

Further complicating matters, a funding shortfall means that millions of Afghan refugees who live in neighboring Pakistan and Iran will not be registered as they were in the past. That will also affect the Pashtun turnout, because many villagers in insecure southern areas have fled across the border.

Violence has already marred the voter registration process, and many fear there could be wider bloodshed on polling day. Many Afghans, like Haji Kabeer, are frightened to bring their relatives, especially women, to the polling stations.

"In the current circumstances, members of my tribe living in the town of Gardez can vote," said Gul Ahmed Ahmedzai, a tribal elder in Paktia province. "But not those in the border areas where the security is poor. What is being done to change that?"

Others say public hostility toward the Kabul government is an even harder challenge to overcome. Haji Qayyun, a tribal elder in central Logar province, campaigned for Karzai ahead of the 2004 election.

"I told people there would be roads and schools and clinics. It was an easy sell," he said. "But now people come and complain that five years later, they still have nothing. I am finding it hard to convince my people to vote. Not just for Karzai, for anyone."

Regardless of what happens on Aug. 20, any incoming Afghan government will face extraordinary challenges. The Taliban have grown stronger and widened their zone of influence. Opium smuggling has mushroomed, as has violent crime, including kidnapping. The economy remains unstable, and tensions between Afghanistan's ethnic minorities are rising.

Pashtuns make up the largest block of Afghanistan's patchwork of ethnic groups. If millions stay home on polling day, either by choice or because they deem it too dangerous to vote, their disenfranchisement could actually contribute to further instability, by fueling perceptions in the south that Pashtuns have been excluded from the political process. Unfortunately, such perceptions could benefit the Taliban, and they certainly won't bolster the view among Afghans that democracy is the best way forward.

Viewpoint 3

Pakistan's Democratic Transition Affects Its Relationship with the West

Husain Haqqani

In the following viewpoint, a former advisor to two Pakistani prime ministers, Husain Haqqani, provides an analysis of Pakistan's 2008 elections that brought opposition parties to power after a decade of military rule. The essay explores the reasons for the opposition victory and analyzes the likelihood of increased tensions between Pakistan and the United States as the result of the new government. Haqqani is the author of Pakistan: Between Mosque and Military *and is currently the director of the Center for International Relations at Boston University.*

As you read, consider the following questions:

1. What has been the main priority of Pakistan's military leaders, according to the author?
2. What were the two largest parties in Pakistan's parliament after the 2008 elections?
3. According to the viewpoint, will the new civilian government of Pakistan be more or less likely to suppress al Qaeda and the Taliban?

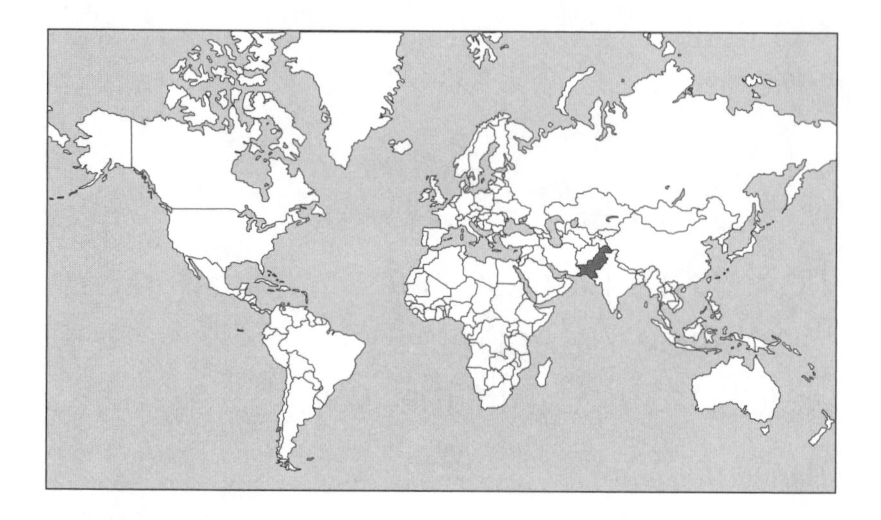

The decision by the opposition parties that won Pakistan's February 18 [2008] parliamentary election to work together offers the hope of bringing democratic stability to a dysfunctional nuclear state. The army has dominated Pakistan's politics for most of its 60-year existence as an independent country. In the past, coup-making generals, like President Pervez Musharraf, have taken advantage of differences among politicians instead of allowing politicians with popular support to negotiate compromises and run the country according to its constitution.

The priority of Pakistan's military rulers has been to create a centralized state, focused on the perceived threat from India, with the help of the United States. US assistance is obtained by allying with Washington's strategic concern of the day, which in turn has led to over-engagement by the military on several fronts.

Pakistan's Problems

Many of Pakistan's problems, such as the influence of jihadi extremists and difficult relations with Afghanistan and India can be traced to the ascendancy of strategic military doctrine at the expense of domestic stability and democratic decision making. All that could now change if the army stays its new course of disengagement from politics and the politicians can work together rather than against each other.

In a clear signal that Pakistan's military recognizes its over-engagement as part of the country's dysfunction, the new commander of the Pakistan army General Ashfaq Kayani ordered his officers to stand aside in the election process. The army's refusal to stuff ballot boxes in favor of Musharraf's political allies led to the two major opposition parties—the center-left Pakistan Peoples Party (PPP) led by Benazir Bhutto's widower Asif Zardari and the center-right Pakistan Muslim League (PML-N) led by former Prime Minister Nawaz Sharif—emerging as the two largest parties in the new parliament.

The Islamist parties were swept aside in a resurgence of the secular center, including the re-emergence of the nationalist Awami National Party (ANP) as the major political force in the Pashtun areas along the Afghan border.

Even after the humiliating defeat of his political allies, whom he supported in every fair or foul way possible until Election Day, Musharraf refuses to step down as president. The opposition, on the other hand, has agreed on a common minimum platform that aims at restoring the Pakistani constitution, rehabilitating its judiciary and moving towards national reconciliation.

Political Problems

Pakistan is a nation in need of healing. The last year has highlighted the many fissures that have festered below the surface for years. Musharraf's rule, and the constant machinations of Pakistan's security services in every aspect of the nation's life, has proved to be divisive. For example, opinion polls show that a clear majority of Pakistanis suspects the security services or Musharraf's political allies, not al Qaeda or the Taliban, for the assassination of Benazir Bhutto [in December

2007]. An elected government that functions in a transparent manner could help lessen widespread mistrust between Pakistan's state and society.

In the recent elections, Pakistan's politicians scored a major victory against what is euphemistically called "the establishment" in Pakistan. But the battle between "the establishment" and the politicians is far from over. "The establishment," made up of politicized generals, intelligence officials and Pakistan's managerial class—bankers, civil servants, some overseas businessmen, beneficiaries of the World Bank and the International Monetary Fund—will not give up easily. Soon there could be rumors of corruption and mismanagement to discredit the elected leadership and a concerted effort to create rifts among them.

Pakistan is a nation in need of healing. The last year has highlighted the many fissures that have festered below the surface for years.

A future government of national unity led by elected politicians would almost certainly try and end the political role of intelligence services. For too long, an all-powerful intelligence community has run—and most observers would agree, ruined—Pakistan by fixing elections, dividing parties and buying off politicians.

Terrorism and Democracy in Pakistan

If the politicians prevail, the war against terrorism would be fought to eliminate out-of-control jihadi groups previously nurtured or tolerated by the Pakistani state, not to secure additional funding from the US. Zardari and Sharif have different levels of commitment to eliminating the jihadis. Having lost his wife to terrorism, Zardari understands that terrorism is a threat to Pakistan whereas Sharif still considers the war against terrorism as an American project. But no one in

"Pakistan's Musharraf would like to be a king," cartoon by David Brown, www.CartoonStock.com. Copyright © David Brown. Reproduction rights obtainable from www.CartoonStock.com.

Pakistan's new political center wants to continue running the risk of calibrating extremist groups for the sake of enhancing the country's global strategic significance, as Musharraf has continuously done since 9/11 [the September 11, 2001, terrorist attacks on the United States].

An elected Pakistani government might be less amenable, say, to requests for rendition of Pakistani citizens. But it would almost certainly be interested in rooting out al Qaeda and stopping cross-border Taliban terrorism in Afghanistan. The civilians would also seek a clearer strategy against militant Talibanization within Pakistan, particularly because they have a popular mandate in the form of electoral rejection of Islamists.

The PPP's Zardari has repeatedly stated in interviews that he considers normalization of relations with India a priority because "Pakistan cannot move on without normal ties with India." As prime minister, Sharif had initiated the peace process with India after both countries' nuclear tests in 1998, yet that came to an abrupt halt when army commander Musharraf started the Kargil war over Jammu and Kashmir. After initial confrontation, Musharraf as president has come around to managing a relatively quiet relationship with Pakistan's larger South Asian neighbor.

During the run-up to the recent elections, none of the major political parties highlighted Pakistan's dispute with India over Kashmir. That raises expectations of a political consensus on developing normal relations with India without insisting on prior resolution of the Kashmir issue. In the past, any politician seeking friendly ties with India has faced criticism from rivals seeking to tap into anti-India sentiment within Pakistan.

A "Grand National Compromise"

The need of the hour in Pakistan is a "grand national compromise" that brings to an end the vilification and demonization of some politicians, restores the military's prestige and ends its political role, limits the intelligence agencies to external security functions and results in a government that unites the Pakistani nation against terrorism and disintegration. Pakistan's foreign policy also needs to be reoriented towards friendlier relations with Pakistan's immediate neighbors instead of being centered merely on scoring points in distant major world capitals. For this to happen, politicians and the permanent state apparatus must become partners, bringing to an end the subordinate relationship that Musharraf had created with handpicked politicians.

If the anti-Musharraf parties can work together and the army's neutrality keeps Musharraf from rocking the boat by undermining the system again, Pakistan could be run according to its constitution. An independent judiciary and a free media would then become the guardians against abuse of power by elected officials. Corruption would probably continue as it has for years, but would be dealt with by the courts and the voters, not by coups d'état. Musharraf has a few days to decide whether he wants to become part of the Grand National Compromise, salvage some respect, and voluntarily give up power. Or he could remain the major wound that must be dealt with before the healing of Pakistan can begin.

VIEWPOINT 4

Nepal's Democracy Needs Support from the International Community

Manjushree Thapa

Manjushree Thapa argues in the following viewpoint that states such as the United States, India, and the United Kingdom were partially responsible for the 2005 coup that briefly ended democracy in Nepal because of their financial and military support of the monarchy. She further contends that Nepal needs substantial aid from the outside world to institutionalize democracy in the country. Thapa is a Nepalese translator and author of works such as Forget Kathmandu: An Elegy for Democracy.

As you read, consider the following questions:

1. What percentage of the Nepalese economy is provided by the international community in the form of foreign aid and assistance?
2. Who led the military coup in Nepal in 2005?
3. What does the author contend are the four main challenges facing pro-democracy political parties in Nepal?

The international reaction following King Gyanendra's military coup on 1 February 2005 has been mostly heartening for Nepalis. Until that date, we felt doomed to be character

Manjushree Thapa, "Democracy in Nepal and the 'International Community,'" *Open Democracy.net*, May 3, 2005. Reproduced by permission.

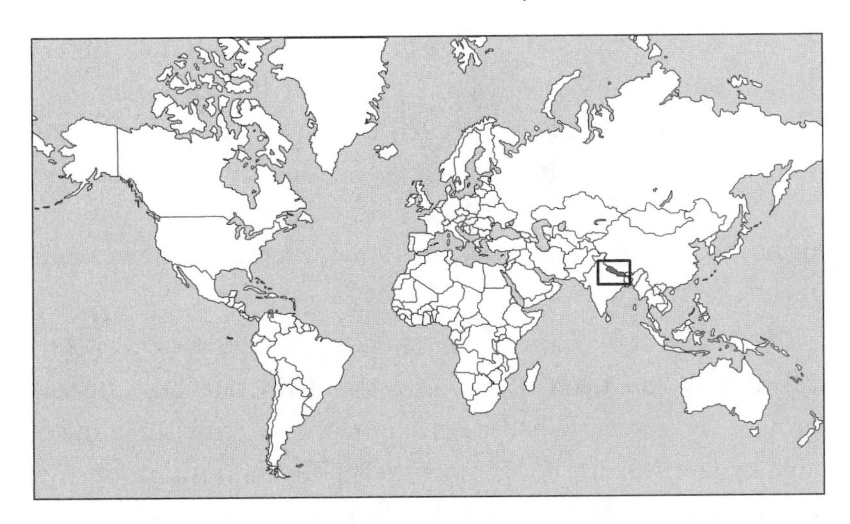

ised as simple, happy mountain folks inhabiting a Shangri-La, who deserved to be ruled by a deity-king, no matter how unjust. Maoist insurgency tended to be viewed as an anachronism, even fey: trouble in paradise. Meanwhile, Nepal's real story—the decades-long (and continuing) struggle to establish and retain democracy—seemed destined to be overlooked. It was just not picturesque.

Nepal and the World

But the world's condemnation of King Gyanendra's military coup has made Nepalis feel that we are not being abandoned at this, the most traumatic and transformational era in our history. Still, Nepalis are wary about the international community's trustworthiness, for any vestigial commitment to democracy in Nepal it has shown in the past has proved fickle.

In part this unreliability is because the outside world simply could not understand Nepal after democracy was won in 1990. It has been difficult enough for Nepalis to clarify this chaotic period even to ourselves. We were not prepared for the challenges of democracy. There were no democratic institutions, and very little democratic practice in either public or private spheres in 1990. The caste structure—with the Chhetri, Bahun and "high-caste" Newar groups at the top—remained rigidly in place. It was widely felt that any move in the direction of equal rights for women would destroy Nepali culture. Any mention of ethnic rights could be met with accusations of harbouring separatist, anti-national, even treasonous sentiments.

This was the legacy of the closed, pre-1990 system. Political parties had been illegal, and could operate only underground. Free speech had been banned, and criticism punishable by law. No one could state their political position openly; communication took place either in tight circles, amid the fear of informers and infiltrators, or via secret messages embedded in public discourse.

The outside world simply could not understand Nepal after democracy was won in 1990.

In this paranoid atmosphere, political activists with liberal, socialist and (various) Communist ideologies tended to remain segregated from and mistrustful of one another.

This stifling polity almost guaranteed that when their time came to govern, the parties would stumble. So it proved: when the ruling Nepali Congress Party abandoned socialism for capitalism under pressure from the World Bank and the IMF [International Monetary Fund] after 1990, the largest opposition party—the Communist Party of Nepal [Unified Marxist-Leninist (UML)]—awkwardly tacked its old-style communism onto free-market economics without rejecting its strain of totalitarianism, as its Indian equivalents were to do. Nepali political parties did not worry at that stage about a comeback by monarchist and military forces, far less an unimaginable Maoist insurgency.

Nepal and Democratization

As a result of this unresolved adaptation to new realities, they muddled endlessly. In the early 1990s, one government after another fell to selfish power grabs, petty infighting and personality-based factionalism; corruption scandals proliferated; parliamentary sessions grew raucous even as street demonstrations, closures and strikes grew. All the major parties eventually split. The accumulated result was to block the progressive social and political reforms that Nepali people desperately needed.

Despite this, the democratic environment did allow lawyers, journalists, businesses and other professional groups to establish themselves. Unions, pressure groups and special interest groups formed. Activism flourished; among the new social movements were those campaigning for the rights of women, *Dalit* [groups considered to be of lower class and often ostracized by the larger population], ethnic groups, and gays.

In the early 1990s, one government after another fell to selfish power grabs, petty infighting and personality-based factionalism; corruption scandals proliferated; parliamentary sessions grew raucous even as street demonstrations, closures and strikes grew.

Such fragile democratic institutions and practices had barely found their footing when the Communist Party of Nepal (Maoist) went underground and launched their armed insurgency in 1996. The Maoist demands were for an all-party interim government to be formed, followed by elections to a constituent assembly, and the creation of a new, republican constitution.

These demands had their roots in the 1940s, when republicanism had begun to grow and Nepali political parties were expressing aspirations to a new constitutional, democratic order. Fifty years on, however, the parties chose to be intimidated rather than inspired by the return of these aspirations in a new guise. To debate the demands seriously would require overcoming complacency and genuinely soul-searching for their own ideological commitments. It was so much easier to do what they did: move rightward.

The Maoist Insurgency

As the Maoist insurgency escalated, Congress-UML governments enforced press censorship, suspended civil rights, and imposed a brutal counterinsurgency—eventually deploying the Royal Nepal[ese] Army—costing thousands of civilian lives. These parties passed the Terrorist and Disruptive Acts Ordinance, which made it possible to arrest people based merely on the suspicion that they were Maoists. In 2001 alone, more than 100 journalists were arrested. Amid vicious infighting and factionalism—intensified in the wake of the royal massacre of June 2001—these parties moved from boycotting an entire session of parliament to eventually dismissing parliament without making the necessary preparations for elections in the war-torn countryside.

A Friendless People

The machinations of the political parties caused a constitutional crisis in 2002, leaving King Gyanendra to take advantage. In October 2002 he dismissed the elected prime minister and established his own cabinet of handpicked palace loyalists. His ostensible purpose was to ease the crisis; he even cited Article 127 of the constitution in justification. This convinced very few Nepalis; people and press responded with street protests and strong denunciations against a return to monarchical rule. The king's takeover was dubbed a "royal regression".

But the international community—diplomats, and monetary and aid agencies—was greatly relieved. Political analysts have generally viewed Nepal's travails as a standoff between three major powers: the king/military (or palace), the political parties, and the Maoists. Hari Roka, a political analyst, has added to this troika a fourth power: the international community, whose diplomats and aid industrialists supply more than 60% of the national budget and often hold more sway over Nepal's governance than Nepalis themselves.

These representative individuals were often genuinely disgusted with the ineptitude of the democratic political parties, and concerned about the growing strength of the Maoist insurgency. But unlike Nepalis, they lacked any memory of life under absolute monarchy: somehow, in their minds, the king was a unifying force for Nepal. They threw their considerable weight behind him. India, the United Kingdom and the United States all welcomed his takeover. Aid, including military aid, continued and even grew.

To put it bluntly, the international community funded his military coup. Most complicit were India, the UK and the US, which together had supplied aid to the Royal Nepal[ese] Army despite its widespread and systematic human rights abuses.

So Nepalis were stuck with a king who had transgressed his constitutional remit. He dismissed cabinet after cabinet, all the while laying the grounds for his final ascendancy to power. This he achieved on 1 February 2005. Before that, he approached the embassies of the three "friendly" countries to gauge their reactions. They—or so they have latterly claimed—unanimously advised the king not to conduct a military coup.

But he did. And only then did it become apparent to the international community that in 2002 it had done no more than help the king buy time, and make the necessary preparations for 1 February 2005. To put it bluntly, the international

Nepal's Return to Democracy

The decade-old armed conflict took a decisive turn with the signing of the 12-point understanding on November 22, 2005, by the Seven Party Alliance (SPA) and the Chairperson of the Communist Party of Nepal (Maoist) for calling for a peaceful agitation against the autocracy of the king and also for holding election to a Constituent Assembly (CA). Although the king sought the legality of his autocratic rule and approval from the international community by holding municipal elections on February 8, 2006, the whole electoral exercise ended in fiasco due to the opposition of the Maoists and the SPA.

Accordingly, SPA in cooperation of the Maoists launched a people's peaceful movement, lasting for nineteen days participated by millions of people throughout the country apart from the capital, paralyzing the state machinery forcing the king to make his midnight proclamation on 24 April 2006 relinquishing the executive power of the state which he had usurped violating the provision of the constitution and restoring the sovereignty to the people, reinstating the dissolved House of Representatives (HoR) and forming a democratic government to run the state.

Birendra Prasad Mishra, "Strengths and Weaknesses of the Nepalese Peace Process," Building Bridges for Peace in Nepal, Centre for Economic and Technical Studies, in cooperation with Friedrich-Ebert-Stiftung (FES), October 2009. www.fesnepal.org.

community funded his military coup. Most complicit were India, the UK and the US, which together had supplied aid to the Royal Nepal[ese] Army despite its widespread and systematic human rights abuses.

The World Reaction to the 2005 Coup

It should have been an outrage to the taxpayers of these liberal-democratic countries that they were backing this dirty war. But it was not. Nepal was too far away, and its troubles were nebulous, obscure. So what if the king's government did not release any expenditure reports since 2002? So what if the king's salary increased hugely while many of his people were famished? So what if nobody knew how aid money was really being used? Only the Nepalis were outraged. But we did not matter.

This is why, despite the fact that India, the UK and the US all suspended military aid following the February coup, Nepalis remain suspicious of the international community. Aid is, after all, a cynical industry. There are jobs and contracts on the line for donor countries. The donor countries' need to disburse aid is often greater than the recipient countries' need to obtain it.

Democracy, moreover, is not the aid industry's concern; in fact, democracy often deters the aid industry by forcing greater transparency and accountability in public expenditure. An old Nepal hand (who wishes to remain anonymous) voiced a common wariness to me when he said: "If this had been a *competent* fascist coup, they would have backed it. But it's been an incompetent fascist coup. They're embarrassed by how crude it is."

King Gyanendra himself may pay lip-service to the notion of democracy, but the army, or at least its top brass, have been openly contemptuous of the idea. It has targeted three groups for the worst repression: democratic political leaders, private media, and human rights activists. The military plan appears to be to silence all potential critics before going after the Maoists. This time, nobody will be able to speak out for the civilians who get in the way.

Nepalis' fear now is that military aid might resume, helping to entrench military rule in Nepal. This is clearly what

King Gyanendra hopes. Claiming that cutting off military aid only supports the Maoists, he has been lobbying hard for its resumption—at times begging before India, the UK and the US, at others threatening to ally with China, Pakistan, and even Cuba.

For a few days in late April it appeared that the king would be granted his wish, when the Indian government seemed ready to resume military aid. Indian security concerns over the Maoists were simply too strong, and the country's military was pressing the New Delhi government. But India's government was also opposed by its own left coalition partner and embarrassed by the continuing arrests of political activists in Nepal. Torn between these impulses, it waffled.

Whatever India does, the UK and the US will most likely follow. So far, the UK has generally given non-lethal aid to Nepal's army, while the US has supplied lethal aid as well. But the supply of helicopters from the UK to Nepal shows how deceptive such categories can be: the Royal Nepal[ese] Army has conducted aerial bombing from helicopters for several years, targeting crowds heavily populated by civilians and a few Maoists. "Non-lethal"?

How Can the World Help Nepal?

What the international community must understand now is that if it resumes military aid, it will be actively helping the king derail Nepal's democracy movement, and in time be held accountable for its betrayal.

If it does so, any appeal by the international community for the restoration of civil liberties, or even of democracy, will mean nothing. For once military rule is entrenched in Nepal, it will be near-impossible to return to developing democratic institutions and practice.

Since 1 February [2005], the parties of the democracy movement in Nepal have been scattered and most of their top leaders are imprisoned, under house arrest, or underground. It is extremely hard to regroup under such conditions, but regroup the movement has.

The second- and third-tier cadres of all the parties are coming to the fore in two ways. First, they are voicing the demand for a new constitution via a constituent assembly, thus reclaiming an aspiration their parties had made as early as the 1940s, long before the Maoists appropriated it. Second, they are following the example of student party activists in the past who were often scorned for their advocacy of republicanism. This move is so far cautious, even nervous—for the monarchy looms larger in the lives and imaginations of older generations.

There is some disagreement as to how to form an all-party government. Some parties would prefer to re-establish the parliament that was dismissed in 2002; others prefer to establish a new all-party interim government. But for the most part, the political parties have by a different route reached the same view as the Maoists: Nepal needs a new constitution.

Since 1 February [2005], the parties of the democracy movement in Nepal have been scattered and most of their top leaders are imprisoned, under house arrest, or underground.

The parties have not overcome their ineptitude and indecision, but they are no longer intimidated by the scare of a return to absolute monarchy, of military rule. This conquest of fear obliges them to scale four new challenges: to throw up good leadership possessed of vision; to move beyond the immaturity that is a legacy of living for so many years underground; to sharpen their governance skills; and—most importantly—to bring the Maoists into a peaceful settlement via a new constitution.

All this can happen, albeit slowly, but only if the international community does not help the king and military to derail democracy before the opportunities can be seized. The king's cautious release from prison of two leading communists, Madhav Kumar Nepal and Amrit Bohara, on 1 May is a small but significant step, reflecting the combination of internal opposition to the coup and external pressure.

Democracy is the only option for Nepal. This has been the main struggle for over seventy years. Nepalis are now regrouping to carry on the democracy movement, defying the severe repression and censorship imposed by the king and the military. They deserve support. The only action that the international community can take in good faith is to make a wager on the Nepali people and their democratic future.

VIEWPOINT 5

Democracy Continues to Spread Around the Globe

Globe & Mail

In the following viewpoint, an editorial from the Globe & Mail, *the author argues that democracy and freedom are spreading around the world. The author asserts that global conflict has declined and that democracy has had some spectacular successes since the end of the Cold War in 1989. Nonetheless, some significant challenges remain to the further spread of democracy. The* Globe & Mail *is Canada's largest national newspaper and is generally considered to be centrist to conservative in its editorial stance.*

As you read, consider the following questions:

1. What author argued that liberal democracy and free market capitalism triumphed after the end of the Cold War?
2. According to the viewpoint, what area of the world has made the least progress in democratization?
3. How many people around the world survive on less than $2 per day?

It has been 15 years since Francis Fukuyama made a splash with his sweeping essay "The End of History." In it, the American scholar argued that liberal democracy and free mar-

"Fukuyama Was Right: We've Come a Long Way," *Globe & Mail* (Toronto, Canada), January 1, 2005, p. A16.

kets had won the great ideological battle of the Cold War, ending any real debate about the best system for organizing human societies. The age-old dispute about where history was leading had essentially ended; thus, the end of history.

Critics called him naïve from the start, and recent events seem to have borne them out. Just look at what happened in the past year [2004]. Terrorists and insurgents in Iraq challenged Washington's attempt to spread liberal democracy and free markets to Iraq and, by example, to the rest of the Middle East. Hundreds of thousands of people went hungry and homeless in Sudan, and the triumphant liberal democratic West seemed powerless to save them (though it has responded with greater alacrity to the tragedies created by the tsunamis).

Russia under Vladimir Putin crept back toward the kind of despotism that Mr. Fukuyama claimed had been defeated in 1989. Terrorist attacks from Madrid to Amsterdam to Jakarta to Jeddah signalled the determination of Muslim extremists to halt the spread of Western values. Iran and North Korea thumbed their noses at the West by refusing to give up their pursuit of nuclear weapons.

So much, the critics say, for the end of history.

Fukuyama's Arguments

But step back a few paces and things begin to look a little brighter. Remember, when Mr. Fukuyama talked about the end of history he did not mean to say that bad things would stop happening.

"There would still be a high and perhaps rising level of ethnic and nationalist violence," he wrote, "since those are impulses incompletely played out, even in parts of the post-historical world. Palestinians and Kurds, Sikhs and Tamils, Irish Catholics and Walloons, Armenians and Azeris, will continue to have their unresolved grievances. This implies that terrorism and wars of national liberation will continue to be an important item on the international agenda."

Civil wars are still common, and claim many thousands of lives, but overall the number of armed conflicts has fallen from more than 30 . . . to about 20.

Nor did he argue that bad people would stop challenging the liberal democratic order that was developing. What he said was that the battle over the ideal form of society—capitalist or fascist or Communist—had essentially ended and, as a result, large-scale conflict between nations would become less likely.

This has proved broadly true. Wars between nations, like that between Iraq and a U.S.-led coalition in 2003, are now a rarity. Civil wars are still common, and claim many thousands of lives, but overall the number of armed conflicts has fallen from more than 30 when Mr. Fukuyama wrote to about 20 today. Some particularly ugly wars—in Liberia, Sierra Leone, Angola and Mozambique—have mercifully come to an end.

Terrorism, of course, is still a worldwide threat, and could become much worse if [al Qaeda leader] Osama bin Laden or others like him were to obtain weapons of mass destruction, as they clearly would like. That is one reason why it is so important to confront Iran and North Korea—both with terrorist ties—over their nuclear ambitions. Despite all the disorder and death they have sown, however, Islamic radicals and rogue states still pose a much smaller challenge to the advance of liberal democracy and general peace and security than the Communist bloc did in the Cold War. Democracy, indeed, is now the global norm, and even those countries that don't practise it usually claim to be democratic by their own lights. Last month's [December 2004] demonstrations in Ukraine were yet another example of

Few Contributions

Few contributions to *The National Interest* can have matched the impact of Francis Fukuyama's 1989 proclamation of "The End of History." In that trenchant essay he captured a historical moment and launched a stellar career. Rather less gratifying in the longer run, he also did much to set his stamp on America's national agenda abroad for the next decade and a half. His was a deft inversion of [17th-century British philosopher] John Locke's distant vision: "in the beginning all the world was America." In the End, with the Cold War no more and the dream of socialism vanishing swiftly over the horizon, the world was at last ready to recognize that it had no other eligible destination or option but to do its faltering best to become America. It had to reconcile itself to embracing, on pain of inanition, chaos or barbarism, not America's distinctive culture and self-assurance or its widely envied levels of material comfort, but its hallowed form of government, and above all, its cherished and endlessly honed diagnosis of the special merits of that form.

John Dunn, "Democracy & Its Discontents,"
National Interest Online, *February 23, 2010.*
www.nationalinterest.org.

democracy's power as an idea. More than 44 per cent of the world's people live in free countries, according to the authoritative survey by New York–based Freedom House. That is up from 24 per cent in 1992.

Democracy Around the Globe

Though democracy is spotty in Africa, shaky in parts of Latin America, all but non-existent in the Arab world and outlawed in China, the number of true despots left in the world is down to a handful and the general trend to political liberty is unmistakable. Indonesia, the world's fifth most populous nation, and a predominantly Muslim one at that, completed its transition from dictatorship to democracy in 2004 with a remarkably peaceful and orderly presidential election, a development that leaves it in better shape to deal with the aftermath of the Asian earthquake.

Even in the Middle East, the stoniest ground for democracy, there is a growing realization that the region's backwardness is linked to the lack of freedom. Though the region's autocrats have proven stubbornly resistant to change, they are feeling more and more pressure from the Western world, particularly the United States, to reform. So Mr. Fukuyama was right when he said that democracy, as an idea, has triumphed. He was right about free markets, too. In the constant and natural wrangling among nations about tariffs and quotas and trade deficits, it is easy to forget how far we have come. The average tariff charged by countries on imports fell from 40 per cent after the Second World War to about 5 per cent when Mr. Fukuyama wrote his famous essay. Though the current round of World Trade Organization talks is dragging, there has been more progress since.

More than 44 per cent of the world's people live in free countries. . . . That is up from 24 per cent in 1992.

Partly as a result, world trade has grown enormously over the decades. The process that its critics condemn as globalization has pulled hundreds of millions out of poverty. The process is most obvious in China, which has experienced an economic revolution since opening up its economy in the late 1970s. If many countries have been left behind, it is not through an excess of globalization but through a lack of it. Those that have not fully joined the international trading system inevitably drag behind.

In May [2004], the European Union continued its eastward expansion by taking in 10 new members, most of them former vassals of Moscow.

Democracy's Successes

Mainly as a result of global capitalism's spread, living standards in almost every region of the world have risen. Life expectancy is up, infant mortality down; school enrolment is up, illiteracy down. The number of people living at what the United Nations calls "medium development"—above poverty, but below prosperity—has grown from 1.6 billion to 3.5 billion over the past quarter-century.

That still leaves far too many living in destitution. About 2.7 billion people make less than $2 (U.S.) a day, a scandal in a time of plenty. But there is hope for them, too. India is recording growth rates of 7 per cent a year as the country follows China's example by freeing up its economy.

As free markets and democracy gain ground, the likelihood of conflict has, indeed, diminished. As nations converge around these pillars, they tend to draw together. Look at Europe, where the crumbling of the Iron Curtain made possible a sweeping continental integration. In May [2004], the European Union continued its eastward expansion by taking in 10 new members, most of them former vassals of Moscow.

On the other side of the world, China was negotiating a free-trade pact with its neighbours in Southeast Asia. Despite the bad blood over the U.S.-led invasion of Iraq without the United Nations' approval, global institutions are taking on new, more muscular roles. The North Atlantic Treaty Organization [NATO], once confined simply to the defence of Western Europe, is helping rebuild and pacify shattered Afghanistan. The Organization of American States [OAS], formerly a limp puppet of Washington, now works to keep its members in line when they abuse human rights or flirt with autocracy.

More democracy. More economic freedom. More global integration. These three developments tend to reinforce each other, winding together like the strands of a rope. Freer markets tend to produce more prosperous people who eventually demand more democracy. Democracy tends to produce the conditions—free media, reliable government, the rule of law—that lead to further economic growth. Democratic, prosperous countries tend to get along better (and fight less) than undemocratic ones, so integration proceeds and cooperation grows. Terrorism and Iraq notwithstanding, the world is generally at peace. New technologies such as cellular telephony and biotechnology are spreading around the globe, enriching lives and bringing people closer together.

You don't have to be a Pollyanna to see that, for all its troubles, the world is becoming a safe, freer, better place. Consolidating and spreading the new liberal order that Mr. Fukuyama identified in 1989 is the major project of the 21st century. Despite the undoubted progress of recent years, there are perils aplenty—AIDS, weapons of mass destruction, mass terrorism, rogue nations. But Mr. Fukuyama's essential point remains true. After a 20th century in which ideologies and systems of economic and political organization competed and collided, one system triumphed. The combination of democracy and free markets is the best system people have devised for liberty and prosperity, delivering undreamed-of progress to those parts of the world lucky enough to enjoy them. Now, let's get on with spreading the Fukuyama formula to those who don't.

Periodical Bibliography

The following articles have been selected to supplement the diverse views presented in this chapter.

Erdong Chen	"Taiwan Plays the 'Democracy Card,'" *Asia Times Online*, October 24, 2009. www.atimes.com.
Michael Collins	"China's Confucius and Western Democracy," *Contemporary Review*, June 22, 2008.
Economist	"Forget About Democracy," March 25, 2010.
Mark Frezzo	"Rethinking Human Rights, Development, and Democracy: The Paradox of the UN," *Perspectives on Global Development & Technology*, 2010.
Isabel Hilton	"Desperately Seeking Democracy," *New Statesman*, May 28, 2009.
Johan Lagerkvist	"Chinese Eyes on Africa: Authoritarian Flexibility Versus Democratic Governance," *Journal of Contemporary African Studies*, April 2009.
Heraldo Muñoz	"A Special Partnership with the UN: A Latin American Perspective," *UN Chronicle*, March 2007.
Takaaki Ohta	"Unlocking Democracy?" *Japan Inc.*, Spring 2009.
Michael Petrou	"The End of Democracy?" *Maclean's*, March 3, 2009.
Robert J. Pranger	"American Foreign Policy After Iraq," *Mediterranean Quarterly*, Summer 2008.
Richard Swift	"Getting a Grip on Democracy," *New Internationalist*, March 2010.
Richard Youngs	"Dicing with Democracy," *World Today*, July 2009.

For Further Discussion

Chapter 1

1. Héctor Mondragón explores the impact of U.S. counter-narcotics efforts in Colombia. Does he make a persuasive case that Plan Colombia has not only been ineffective, but also that it has undermined democracy? What could be done to make efforts to suppress the drug trade more effective?
2. According to the viewpoint by Tim Meisburger, democracy is threatened in Thailand. What are the main dangers? Can they be reduced or eliminated?
3. Andrew Aeria asserts that the Malaysian government is endeavoring to suppress democracy. What are the main tactics used by the regime against its domestic opponents? Are these efforts effective in constraining democracy?

Chapter 2

1. In the viewpoint by Agnieszka Graff, what are the principal reasons that the public in Eastern Europe no longer has confidence or trust in nongovernmental organizations? How can that trust be regained?
2. David Newman is very critical of the ways in which Israel discriminates against its Arab citizens. Does the author make a good argument? What are the main weaknesses in the viewpoint?

Chapter 3

1. Anatole Kaletsky questions the actions of the governments of the United States and the United Kingdom. According to his viewpoint, what are the main reasons for the in-

creased role of the government in the economy? What are the main flaws in his argument? What are the main strengths?

2. Jean-Francois Seznec explores how states in the Persian Gulf have grown economically but without a concurrent expansion in equality or individual freedom. What are the main points that Seznec cites to support his arguments?

Chapter 4

1. Joseph Nye asserts that the United States has made a number of mistakes in its efforts to promote democracy. Do you agree with his main points? Why or why not?
2. Husain Haqqani explores some of the ramifications of Pakistan's 2008 transition to democracy. What are the main challenges that the author claims Pakistan currently faces? How will these obstacles affect the country's relations with the international community, especially the United States?

Organizations to Contact

The editors have compiled the following list of organizations concerned with the issues debated in this book. The descriptions are derived from materials provided by the organizations. All have publications or information available for interested readers. The list was compiled on the date of publication of the present volume; the information provided here may change. Be aware that many organizations take several weeks or longer to respond to inquiries, so allow as much time as possible.

Brookings Institution

1775 Massachusetts Avenue NW, Washington, DC 20036
(202) 797-6000 • fax: (202) 536-3623
e-mail: communications@brookings.edu
website: www.brookings.edu

The Brookings Institution was founded in 1927 and is one of the nation's most prominent nonprofit, nonpartisan research centers. It conducts research on both domestic and international issues, including analyses of the strengths and weaknesses of democracy and democratization. Brookings publishes a wide variety of reports on the debate over the utility of democracy at home and abroad. The Brookings Institution Press publishes books that result from the institution's own research and books of a similar nature written by the authors, such as *Toughing It Out on Afghanistan* and *The East Moves West.*

Canadian International Council (CIC)

45 Willcocks Street, Suite 210
Toronto, Ontario M5S 1C7 Canada
(416) 946-7209 • fax: (416) 946-7319
e-mail: info@onlinecic.org
website: www.onlinecic.org

The Canadian International Council (CIC) is a private, nonpartisan institution devoted to research and the dissemination of knowledge on international affairs. The CIC works to bring together academics, public officials, and business leaders to discuss and debate foreign policy, including issues such as democratic transition and promotion. The CIC produces a number of publications, including the prominent journal *International Journal*, which was founded in 1946.

Carnegie Endowment for International Peace
1779 Massachusetts Avenue NW
Washington, DC 20036-2103
(202) 483-7600 • fax: (202) 483-1840
e-mail: info@carnegieendowment.org
website: www.carnegieendowment.org

The Carnegie Endowment for International Peace was founded in 1910 to support international peace and stability. It is an independent, nonprofit research organization that sponsors studies on a range of issues, including international security, globalization, and democracy. Carnegie produces books, policy briefs, reports, working papers, and Web-only commentaries on democracy and its impact on world politics as a dominant political system.

Cato Institute
1000 Massachusetts Avenue NW
Washington, DC 20001-5403
(202) 842-0200 • fax: (202) 842-3490
e-mail: pr@cato.org
website: www.cato.org

The Cato Institute is an American nonprofit, libertarian research body founded in 1977 by Edward H. Crane. The institute advocates for limited government and individual choice in public policy matters. It conducts a range of seminars and conferences, and it publishes a variety of research materials on democracy-building policy. Among its many publications are books; the official blog, Cato@Liberty; *Cato Journal*; and *Cato Policy Report*.

Center for International Policy (CIP)
1717 Massachusetts Avenue NW, Suite 801
Washington, DC 20036
(202) 232-3317 • fax: (202) 232-3440
e-mail: cip@ciponline.org
website: http://ciponline.org

The Center for International Policy (CIP) is a private, left-wing organization founded in 1975 by former diplomats and peace activists. Its mission is to promote U.S. foreign policies that align with, and reflect, democratic values. The group supports research on democratization, human rights, and demilitarization. In addition to several books, CIP regularly publishes short analytical pieces known as *International Policy Reports.*

Center for Strategic & International Studies (CSIS)
1800 K Street NW, Washington, DC 20006
(202) 887-0200 • fax: (202) 775-3199
website: http://csis.org

The Center for Strategic & International Studies (CSIS) was founded in 1962 to provide cutting-edge research on international issues. CSIS is a nonprofit, nonpartisan research body that is currently one of the world's largest and most comprehensive policy think tanks. Its programs and researchers address all areas of global politics, including democracy and democracy promotion. CSIS publishes the influential journal *Washington Quarterly.*

Centre for Independent Studies (CIS)
PO Box 92, St Leonards
NSW 1590 Australia
61 2 9438 4377 • fax: 61 2 9439 7310
e-mail: cis@cis.org.au
website: www.cis.org.au

With offices in Australia and New Zealand, the Centre for Independent Studies (CIS) is a nonprofit research organization founded in 1976 that supports a free enterprise economy and a free society under limited government. CIS facilitates interaction between academics and policy makers on issues important to Australia and the broader Pacific region. It publishes a range of general studies as well as commissioned reports on individual topics, including democracy.

Council on Foreign Relations (CFR)
1777 F Street NW, Washington, DC 20006
(202) 509-8400 • fax: (202) 509-8490
website: www.cfr.org

The Council on Foreign Relations (CFR) was formed in 1921. CFR is a nonpartisan, nonprofit research organization. Its mission is to be a resource on foreign policy issues for business, government, and the public. CFR produces a range of reports, studies, and books, including the journal *Foreign Affairs*. CFR has issued a number of publications on democracy as a tool for American foreign policy.

Democracy Coalition Project
1730 Pennsylvania Avenue NW, 7th Floor
Washington, DC 20006
(202) 721-5630 • fax: (202) 721-5658
e-mail: info@demcoalition.org
website: www.demcoalition.org

The Democracy Coalition Project supports efforts within societies to establish open democratic systems that respect human rights. The coalition was founded in 2001 as an initiative of the Open Society Institute and primarily conducts research and advocacy through the United Nations Human Rights Council.

Freedom House
1301 Connecticut Avenue NW, Floor 6
Washington, DC 20036
(202) 296-5101 • fax: (202) 293-2840
e-mail: info@freedomhouse.org
website: www.freedomhouse.org

Freedom House was founded in 1941 as an independent organization committed to monitoring, measuring, and promoting freedom throughout the world. In assessing the extent to which a country is free, the organization monitors democratic characteristics and human rights in different areas of the world as indicators of the level of democracy. Freedom House provides many forms of support for freedom and democracy through publishing analyses, providing training and support for advocacy groups, and hosting public events related to its cause. It also publishes an annual index of freedom among the nations of the world.

German Council on Foreign Relations
D-10787, Berlin Germany
49(0)30 25 42 31-0 • fax: 49(0)30 25 42 31-16
e-mail: info@dgap.org
website: http://en.dgap.org

The German Council on Foreign Relations (DGAP) is Germany's premier think tank on foreign policy and international relations. It is an independent, nonprofit research body that seeks to contribute to the political process in Germany and to promote Germany's role in the world as a leading democratic world power. DGAP produces a number of publications on democracy at regional and international levels, in both English and German.

International Institute for Democracy and Electoral Assistance (International IDEA)
Strömsborg, Stockholm SE-103 34 Sweden
+46 8 698 37 00 • fax: +46 8 20 24 22
e-mail: info@idea.int
website: www.idea.int

The International Institute for Democracy and Electoral Assistance (International IDEA) is an intergovernmental organization that was founded in 1995. The institute promotes sustainable democratic transitions by providing knowledge about democracy-building projects from all over the world, by assisting political actors in democratic reform, and ultimately by helping to shape democratic policies. International IDEA publishes a comprehensive range of titles, including handbooks, regional and country reports, and more.

International Institute for Strategic Studies (IISS)
Arundel House, 13–15 Arundel Street, Temple Place
London WC2R 3DX England
+44 (0) 20 7379 7676 • fax: +44 (0) 20 7836 3108
website: www.iiss.org

The International Institute for Strategic Studies (IISS) is a nonprofit British institute devoted to the study of international relations and global security. Founded in 1958, the IISS initially focused on nuclear deterrence. Currently it addresses the full range of economic, political, and security issues throughout the world, to include many studies regarding the impact of democracy on the international system and democratization. It has more than twenty-five hundred members in more than one hundred countries. IISS produces a number of publications, including an annual review of world affairs, *Strategic Survey*; a quarterly newsletter, the *ISS News*; and a research series, the Adelphi book series.

National Endowment for Democracy (NED)
1025 F Street NW, Suite 800, Washington, DC 20004
(202) 378-9700 • fax: (202) 378-9407
e-mail: info@ned.org
website: www.ned.org

The National Endowment for Democracy (NED) is a private, nonprofit grant-making foundation dedicated to the growth and strengthening of democratic institutions around the world. Each year, NED issues more than one thousand grants to support the projects of nongovernmental groups working for democratic goals in more than ninety countries. NED's Web site provides access to research, presentations, and articles relating to democratic development.

Organization of American States (OAS)
Seventeenth Street and Constitution Avenue NW
Washington, DC 20006
(202) 458-3000
website: www.oas.org/en

The Organization of American States (OAS) was founded in 1948, though its origins date back to the First International Conference of American States (1889–90). The organization is made up of thirty-five countries of the Americas and is the principal political forum in the Western Hemisphere. The OAS pursues its objectives based on its four pillars: democracy, human rights, security, and development. Its most important publication is *Américas* magazine.

Bibliography of Books

Daron Acemoglu and James A. Robinson — *Economic Origins of Dictatorship and Democracy*. Cambridge, UK: Cambridge University Press, 2006.

Daniele Archibugi — *The Global Commonwealth of Citizens: Toward Cosmopolitan Democracy*. Princeton, NJ: Princeton University Press, 2008.

William Avilés — *Global Capitalism, Democracy, and Civil-Military Relations in Colombia*. Albany, NY: State University of New York Press, 2006.

Leonardo Avritzer — *Democracy and the Public Space in Latin America*. Princeton, NJ: Princeton University Press, 2002.

Terence Ball and Richard Bellamy, eds. — *The Cambridge History of Twentieth-Century Political Thought*. Cambridge, UK: Cambridge University Press, 2003.

Aharon Barak — *The Judge in a Democracy*. Princeton, NJ: Princeton University Press, 2006.

Zbigniew Brzezinski and Brent Scowcroft — *America and the World: Conversations on the Future of American Foreign Policy*. New York: Basic Books, 2008.

Thomas Carothers — *Confronting the Weakest Link: Aiding Political Parties in New Democracies*. Washington, DC: Carnegie Endowment for International Peace, 2006.

Thomas Carothers *Critical Mission: Essays on Democracy Promotion*. Washington, DC: Carnegie Endowment for International Peace, 2004.

Thomas Carothers and Marina Ottaway *Uncharted Journey: Promoting Democracy in the Middle East*. Washington, DC: Carnegie Endowment for International Peace, 2005.

Susan J. Carroll and Richard L. Fox, eds. *Gender and Elections: Shaping the Future of American Politics*. New York: Cambridge University Press, 2010.

Amy Chua *World on Fire: How Exporting Free Market Democracy Breeds Ethnic Hatred and Global Instability*. New York: Anchor Books, 2004.

Gordon Crawford *Foreign Aid and Political Reform: A Comparative Analysis of Democracy Assistance and Political Conditionality*. New York: Palgrave, 2001.

Robert Alan Dahl, Ian Shapiro, and José Antonio Cheibub *The Democracy Sourcebook*. Cambridge, MA: MIT Press, 2003.

Christian Davenport *State Repression and the Domestic Democratic Peace*. New York: Cambridge University Press, 2007.

Jeroen de Zeeuw and Krishna Kumar, eds. *Promoting Democracy in Postconflict Societies*. Boulder, CO: Lynne Rienner Publishers, 2006.

Larry Diamond and Leonardo Morlino	*Assessing the Quality of Democracy.* Baltimore, MD: Johns Hopkins University Press, 2005.
Larry Diamond, Marc F. Plattner, and Daniel Brumberg	*Islam and Democracy in the Middle East.* Baltimore, MD: Johns Hopkins University Press, 2003.
Larry Diamond, Marc F. Plattner, and Philip J. Costopoulos	*World Religions and Democracy.* Baltimore, MD: Johns Hopkins University Press, 2005.
Bob Edwards, Michael W. Foley, and Mario Diani, eds.	*Beyond Tocqueville: Civil Society and the Social Capital Debate in Comparative Perspective.* Hanover, NH: University Press of New England, 2001.
Omar G. Encarnación	*The Myth of Civil Society: Social Capital and Democratic Consolidation in Spain and Brazil.* New York: Palgrave Macmillan, 2003.
Melissa Estok, Neil Nevitte, and Glenn Cowan	*The Quick Count and Election Observation: An NDI Handbook for Civic Organizations and Political Parties.* Washington, DC: National Democratic Institute for International Affairs, 2002.
Francis Fukuyama	*The End of History and the Last Man.* New York: Free Press, 2006.
Daniel J. Galvin	*Presidential Party Building: Dwight D. Eisenhower to George W. Bush.* Princeton, NJ: Princeton University Press, 2010.

Richard Gillespie and Richard Youngs, eds.	*The European Union and Democracy Promotion: The Case of North Africa.* Portland, OR: Frank Cass Publishers, 2002.
Robert E. Goodin	*Reflective Democracy*. Oxford, UK: Oxford University Press, 2003.
Zoltan L. Hajnal	*America's Uneven Democracy: Race, Turnout, and Representation in City Politics*. Cambridge: Cambridge University Press, 2010.
Morton H. Halperin, Joseph T. Siegle, and Michael M. Weinstein	*The Democracy Advantage: How Democracies Promote Prosperity and Peace*. New York: Routledge, 2010.
David Held	*Models of Democracy*. Malden, MA: Polity, 2006.
Marcel Hénaff and Tracy B. Strong, eds.	*Public Space and Democracy*. Minneapolis: University of Minnesota Press, 2001.
Paul K. Huth and Todd L. Allee	*The Democratic Peace and Territorial Conflict in the Twentieth Century*. Cambridge, UK: Cambridge University Press, 2002.
Ronald Inglehart and Christian Welzel	*Modernization, Cultural Change, and Democracy: The Human Development Sequence*. Cambridge, UK: Cambridge University Press, 2005.
Farrukh Iqbal and Jong-Il You, eds.	*Democracy, Market Economics, and Development: An Asian Perspective*. Washington, DC: World Bank, 2001.

Kathleen Hall Jamieson, ed.	*Electing the President, 2008: The Insiders' View*. Philadelphia: University of Pennsylvania Press, 2009.
John Kane	*Between Virtue and Power: The Persistent Moral Dilemma of U.S. Foreign Policy*. New Haven, CT: Yale University Press, 2008.
David Karol	*Party Position Change in American Politics: Coalition Management*. Cambridge, UK: Cambridge University Press, 2009.
L. Ali Khan	*A Theory of Universal Democracy: Beyond the End of History*. The Hague, Netherlands: Kluwer Law International, 2003.
Alexander T.J. Lennon, ed.	*Democracy in U.S. Security Strategy: From Promotion to Support*. Washington, DC: Center for Strategic and International Studies Press, 2009.
Michael Loriaux	*European Union and the Deconstruction of the Rhineland Frontier*. Cambridge, UK: Cambridge University Press, 2008.
Michael Mandelbaum	*The Case for Goliath: How America Acts as the World's Government in the 21st Century*. New York: PublicAffairs, 2005.
Lee Marsden	*Lessons from Russia: Clinton and US Democracy Promotion*. Aldershot, UK: Ashgate, 2005.

David S. Mason — *The End of the American Century.* Lanham, MD: Rowman & Littlefield, 2009.

Sarah E. Mendelson and John K. Glenn, eds. — *The Power and Limits of NGOs: A Critical Look at Building Democracy in Eastern Europe and Eurasia.* New York: Columbia University Press, 2002.

Dana D. Nelson — *Bad for Democracy: How the Presidency Undermines the Power of the People.* Minneapolis: University of Minnesota Press, 2008.

Ronald J. Pestritto and William J. Atto, eds. — *American Progressivism: A Reader.* Lanham, MD: Lexington Books, 2008.

Robert D. Putnam — *Making Democracy Work: Civic Traditions in Modern Italy.* Princeton, NJ: Princeton University Press, 1993.

Peter J. Schraeder, ed. — *Exporting Democracy: Rhetoric vs. Reality.* Boulder, CO: Lynne Reiner Publishers, 2002.

Gene Sharp — *From Dictatorship to Democracy: A Conceptual Framework for Liberation.* Boston, MA: Albert Einstein Institution, 2008.

Jackie Smith — *Social Movements for Global Democracy.* Baltimore, MD: Johns Hopkins University Press, 2008.

Torbjörn Tännsjö — *Global Democracy: The Case for a World Government.* Edinburgh: Edinburgh University Press, 2008.

James Traub	*The Freedom Agenda: Why America Must Spread Democracy (Just Not the Way George Bush Did)*. New York: Farrar, Straus & Giroux, 2008.
Carolyn M. Warner	*The Best System Money Can Buy: Corruption in the European Union*. Ithaca, NY: Cornell University Press, 2007.
Leonard Weinberg, ed.	*Democratic Responses to Terrorism*. New York: Routledge, 2008.
Laurence Whitehead	*Emerging Market Democracies: East Asia and Latin America*. Baltimore, MD: Johns Hopkins University Press, 2002.
Fareed Zakaria	*The Future of Freedom: Illiberal Democracy at Home and Abroad*. New York: W.W. Norton & Co., 2007.
Charles L. Zelden	*Bush v. Gore: Exposing the Hidden Crisis in American Democracy*. Lawrence, KS: University of Kansas Press, 2010.

Index

Geographic headings and page numbers in **boldface** refer to viewpoints about that country or region.

D

E

H

I

J

K

O

P

Q

R

S

V

W